DON'T THROW AWAY YOUR CONFIDENCE

YOUR REWARD IS CLOSER THAN YOU REALIZE

J. Richard Evans, Sr.

J. Richard Evans Sr.

Don't Throw Away Your Confidence
Copyright © 2014 by Restoration Publishing

All rights reserved. No part of this book may be reproduced or transmitted in any form or by any means without written permission from the author.

ISBN 978-0-9905283-0-2

Dedication

I would like to dedicate this book to those who have been an inspiration to me throughout my life, especially during the difficult times. To my mother, from the cradle you have instilled in me the will to reach beyond my limitations and outside the confines of my present situation. To my wife, you see beyond my faults, and believe in me and my ability to achieve and accomplish my goals, this is why I love you for life. To my children who allow me to simply be "Dad." To my congregation, I will never give up on you, so kindly return the favor. To my spiritual parents, Apostle Wayne T. Jackson and Dr. Beverly Y. Jackson, you embraced me when I was broken and nursed me back to health, I am forever grateful. I love you all.

J. Richard Evans Sr.

DON'T THROW AWAY YOUR CONFIDENCE

Table of Contents

Dedication iii

Foreword vii

Preface ix

Introduction xi

Chapter 1
Don't Throw Away Your Confidence 1

Chapter 2
Spiritual Warriors for God 31

Chapter 3
Casting Down Strongholds 47

Chapter 4
Spiritual Boot Camp 75

Chapter 5
God Will Sustain You 105

Chapter 6
All Sustaining Power 127

Chapter 7
Don't Be Insecure 147

Chapter 8
Don't Quit...GET YOUR REWARD 163

J. Richard Evans Sr.

Foreword

When Bishop Evans first approached me to write the foreword to "Don't Throw Away Your Confidence," I readily and enthusiastically agreed. I did so not because I was the editor, but because of what a difference this book has made in my life during the editing process and my fervent belief that the information contained herein is vital for every Christian, but particularly for men.

In my 20s I joined the Marine Corps, an organization that everyone would agree excels in inspiring confidence in a person. Following my time in the Marine Corps I pastored a small country church for over four years. Eventually God would lead me to found JM publications and edit Christian books. I have edited books for Christians not just in America, but in many foreign countries including Australia, Canada, China as well as authors from Nigeria, Mauritania, Mexico and Venezuela.

With such a background one would assume that I would have no problem in the area of confidence and self-worth. I have read literally hundreds of books in my lifetime and edited close to 30 books but there are only a handful that I can honestly say have changed my life. Bishop Evans' book is one such work.

J. Richard Evans Sr.

During a time of change in our family's circumstances in having to move from our house of 12 years the devil was able to get into my mind and cause me to doubt my confidence in God despite his being faithful to take care of us all these years.

During this time when I was editing the book I came to a particular passage that said, "So the enemy sets out to systematically sift us. Some people's salvation is just one late mortgage payment away."

It was then that a feeling of great peace came over me as I stood in humble awe at God's perfect timing in having me edit that particular passage at that exact moment.

I have no doubt if God can use this book to lift a preacher with nearly 50 years on this earth and decades of service for Him, that he can use it in the life of all who read it if they are willing to approach it with a teachable spirit.

I pray that you would wisely approach it with an attitude of "open thou mine eyes, that I may behold wondrous things out of thy law" (Psalms 119:18).

Pastor Jack Minor,
Founder, JM Publications

Preface

I wrote this book after a season in my life when I felt like quitting and giving up. During this time I sought the Lord and he literally heard my cry. I've learned that through trials and suffering, come maturity and confidence. Not confidence in the flesh, but confidence that the Lord would always be there to both comfort me and guide me. There is an inner strength that we have as believers that at times needs to be awakened. The Lord awakened something in me that I've learned to live by, and that is this, "all things are possible to them that believe" (Mark 9:23).

J. Richard Evans Sr.

Introduction

It is my sincere prayer that all who read this book will be inspired to continue to believe the Lord concerning the strength and conviction of their "inner man," the Holy Spirit. Often we make the mistake of confusing confidence in the Word of God concerning our lives with a spirit of pride. However, if you read scripture, you discover that the Bible is replete with examples of the teaching and instruction through the "word" on being confident in your God given abilities to accomplish your goals. Therefore, be encouraged, move forward, and receive your reward.

J. Richard Evans Sr.

Chapter 1

Don't Throw Away Your Confidence

"So do not throw away your confidence; it will be richly rewarded. You need to persevere so that when you have done the will of God, you will receive what he has promised." (Hebrews 10:35-36 NIV)

The dictionary defines confidence as believing in your own or someone else's abilities for success. The Bible warns us to be careful about becoming overconfident because it could cause us to put our faith in ourselves rather than God.

"Remember those early days after you first saw the light? Those were the hard times! Kicked around in public, targets of every kind of abuse—some days it was you, other days your friends. If some friends went to prison, you stuck by them. If some enemies broke in and seized your goods, you let them go with a smile, knowing they couldn't touch your real treasure. Nothing they did bothered you, nothing set you back. So don't throw it all away now. You were sure of yourselves then. It's still a sure thing! But you need to stick it out, staying with God's plan so you'll be there for the promised completion. It won't be long now, he's on the way; he'll show up most any minute. But anyone who is right with me thrives on loyal trust; if he cuts

and runs, I won't be very happy. But we're not quitters who lose out. Oh, no! We'll stay with it and survive, trusting all the way." (Hebrews 10:32-39 The Message)

Don't throw away your confidence. After all you've come through, after all you've mastered concerning the things of God, there will still inevitably come a time in your life where you're going to be confronted with something that will cause you to lose heart, and even come close to fainting. The Bible wouldn't have warned us about this if it weren't true. No matter how strong you become and how knowledgeable you become in the things of God, no matter how many accolades you receive in life, no matter how many rewards, no matter how many people pump you up and pat you on the back and tell you how great you are, you're still going to confront something in life that's going to cause you to feel like quitting. It will cause you to feel like giving up and even question your walk with God; it will cause you to question everything, including whether there is even a God or not. **Regardless of the trials you face, there is a God.**

I was speaking to someone just the other day about a situation that happened in our city where a firefighter, who was a Christian, lost his life putting out a fire and leaving behind a wife and six children. When this happens it is normal to ask how this kind of tragedy can happen. I faced the same questions myself when a dear Christian friend of mine, who would give you the shirt off his back, was killed by someone who didn't value his life. All I can say is we don't have all the answers, and may never have them this side of glory, but we can find peace in that although they lost their lives, they did not lose their souls.

When we find ourselves with unanswered questions, what do we do? I've been there myself where I have said "C'mon God, I've been praying and fasting. I go to church. I'm a good father. I do the best I can to be a good husband. I do the best I can to provide for the church and the members that I have. I'm doing the best I can to be a good son, and yet things are not going the way I think they should go." I know many people who are bold enough to talk to God like that. Now I don't go in with an attitude, because of my reverence for God, but I'm not afraid to ask him the hard questions because I need to have an answer. "Why am I hungry? Why do I sometimes get sick? Why is it that I can lay hands on people to be healed, but I'm still taking medicine? Why can I pray for other people's marriages to be restored, and here I am still going to counseling?" **Have you ever been in a position where you ask the question "Why?"** This doesn't mean I don't trust God; it means I don't understand. I'm not saying God, I don't trust you, I'm saying I don't understand. There are times in my life when my confidence begins to wane because of the hits I find myself taking in life. How is it that I can lay out a pattern of success for the people that I pastor, or the people I'm raising in my own house, but at every turn they seem to fail or face failure? Right when you think you have things figured out something happens that makes you question it all over again. Has anyone here ever been thrown a curve ball?

You're in the fight of your life, so fight to win!

What separates an ordinary boxer from an exceptional one is not how many wins he has, but the quality of his opponents. They both have physical skills, however, the champion has the mental capacity, along with skill, to execute a strategy and secure a victory. People admire the great boxers like Muhammad Ali or others like him for their ability to bounce back after a loss. If you obtain any amount of success in life, your focus becomes maintaining long-term success while overcoming failure.

I've seen boxers that were great, but after suffering a knockout they were never the same. It did something to them mentally even though physically they were just fine. Mentally they could not get over the hump of being knocked out and now every time they see an opening to throw a punch, they hesitate for fear of being knocked out again. Being knocked out means you were hit with a blow in which you were unable to rise and resume fighting. Maybe you

DON'T THROW AWAY YOUR CONFIDENCE

simply got caught off guard. You didn't see it coming. You didn't foresee the power that was going to be on the blow you took. You thought you could handle it and felt you were prepared, but it knocked you completely out. You may have suffered a loss physically, but mentally and spiritually you're still a champion. **Scripture says if a person faints in the day of adversity, their strength is small.** There are many factors that can cause a person to lose confidence. Of course, we are not supposed to have confidence in the flesh, however, you don't want to lose confidence in the abilities God has given you.

"For greater is He that is in me than he that is in the world." (I John 4:4)

"I can do all things through Christ who strengthens me." (Philippians 4:13)

So I have a responsibility in God to accomplish some things, *"for faith without works is dead"* (James 2:20).

Our enemy understands the power of discouragement, so his job is to break you down. He says, "I cannot get them to sin, so I'm going to get them busy. I'm going to get them tired, I'm going to get them frustrated and confused. I'm going to work on them and WEAR THEM DOWN." The devil cannot wear you out, but he can wear you down. The Bible says that no weapon formed against you will prosper, so the enemy has to work on you to get you to the place that you quit because, according to scripture, he cannot do anything to you that you don't give him permission to do. Knowing this, he wants to frustrate you and wear you down so that you give up.

So the Scripture says, "do not throw away your confidence." There was a time when you first got saved and you were so sensitive to the Holy Ghost that you were able to forget things that came at you, and were able to let stuff go. During this time you handled things differently because you were sensitive to the things of God, but over time you became numb. Some of us have gone through so much heartache and pain that the only way to cope with it is to be numb. I know that the world has told you being numb and apathetic are a sign of strength, but the fact of the matter is, that is a lie. We're numb because we're walking around injured with wounds that have never truly healed, and we disguise them by saying "we're just being strong."

The body has a natural ability to cause pain to subside. There is a chemical release in your body called serotonin. When you scream, serotonin is released and it causes the pain in your body to subside. So if God put natural mechanisms in your body to either cause you not to go through so much pain or instead be able to endure it, then there has to be some spiritual painkillers as well. They that weep... **they that sow in tears will reap in joy**. So you see, there are some spiritual mechanisms in place that will keep you from falling, to keep you from losing heart and fainting.

When you were first saved God blessed you because you were still a baby. When I was a baby I needed cartoons on television. I couldn't fathom a life without cartoons, but this is because I was a baby. At Christmastime I expected a gift under the tree from Santa, regardless of whether I deserved it or not. I say all this to say that when we first met God, he blessed us in order to encourage us to not lose our enthusiasm in the things of God or his way of doing things.

As we begin to mature there is no longer a need for God to put gifts under your tree all of the time. You are supposed to be grown up. You're going to have to make adjustments because things are going to change.

That's what the scripture is saying. Just because your life is changing, doesn't mean that you walk away from all that God has taught you about how to deal with issues. You still need to be excited about the blessings of God and the things that bring you joy in Christ and not let life make you bitter. That's why the scripture says, "do not wax cold." Now that is a challenge because we have that nagging question, "Why did this happen to me? Why did this happen to them?"

There are so many people in Christendom that walk away from God because a loved one died and they didn't know why. Again, I can understand the natural reasons why they would feel this way, but the scripture commands us to walk in the Spirit, because if I walk in the Spirit I will not fulfill the lusts of the flesh.

So this text is saying "I don't want you to lose heart." Do you know what happens when people lose heart? The Bible says **if we lose heart or if we faint, we don't receive the harvest**. I don't know about you, but I've come too far to miss out on the harvest.

Confidence is belief in your own or in someone else's ability. This is why the enemy wants to attack the reputation of preachers and other leaders. The enemy's job is to tear down the person's name. In the church, every attack is focused on the leader because the scripture says, "strike the Shepherd, and the sheep will scatter" (Zechariah 13:7). In your personal life, the enemy will attack you with something they know you're attached to. This is to get your attention. Whether it be your family, your children, or your job, these are things you care about that he can use to divert your attention away from God.

When people want to hurt you and can't get to you, they typically go after someone you love. This is more hurtful than a direct attack because you have to struggle with the fact that if it weren't for you this wouldn't have happened to them; making it a mental as well as a physical attack. This attack messes with your mind and emotions as well as your body, your will, your strength etc.

So the enemy wants to attack the essence of who you are. He attacks you at the core of your identity. He's after what you are on the inside. The Bible says, *"out of the abundance of your heart, your mouth speaks"* (Matthew 12:34) and *"as a man thinketh in his heart, so is he"* (Proverbs 23:7), so the enemy seeks to attack who you really are. He knows who you really are. Yes he does. He knows you better than you know yourself. The only person that knows you better than Satan is God. Once you become a person of significance in the Kingdom he begins to check you out. He's looking for an opportunity. Satan desires to have you, to sift you like wheat. He strategically agitates you. Have you ever seen the television show Gold Rush where they sift dirt, rocks, and water looking for gold? They put everything in a bowl or a machine and shake it until everything they didn't want was gone and nothing was left except what they were looking for. Do you know this is similar to what is happening to you? All that stuff the enemy is shaking he really doesn't want, but he's got to shake it off of you to get to what he wants. *There's something about you that is valuable that the enemy wants so that God can't have it.*

We are much more valuable than we think we are. It's true that we are not to think of ourselves more highly than we ought to think, but you need to recognize the value of who you are. You are valuable enough that Jesus died for you. Sometimes we lock up our earthly treasures and take more steps to ensure their protection than we do our own salvation. We are more protective of the car we drive and more selective of the shoes we wear than about whether the person we partner with could or could not cost us our salvation. I've seen people spend more time in a shoe store trying to pick out a pair of shoes than they did deciding who they were going to sleep with that night for that one night stand. That is a person who doesn't recognize their value. They don't know who they are.

So the enemy sets out to systematically sift us. Some people's salvation is just one late mortgage payment away. Some people's walk with God or lack thereof, is just one repossession away. If their car gets repossessed, they quit God. If they're given an eviction letter, they're done.

So the enemy seeks to find your weakness. You make a decision that you're not going to sleep around or you're not going to party. Rest assured the enemy will check you out to find out if you can truly stand firm in your decision and convictions. Satan desires to have you. He's determined to wear you down and find your vulnerability. He wears you out

DON'T THROW AWAY YOUR CONFIDENCE

until what you thought was your strength appears to be gone. Do you think you are too much of a prayer warrior for him to attack you this way? He will work you over and wear you out until he finds out that you're holding onto more than God, and then he begins to work on that because that's really your god. He finds out where your heart really is. The sifting and shaking is designed to tear your confidence up. He systematically sets out to destroy your confidence because he knows that if you lose your confidence, you will eventually give up and then you will faint and won't get the promise.

Galatians says don't be weary while doing good because in due season you will reap if you don't faint. Don't lose heart. Don't lose confidence. Don't lose heart in the good things you are doing because you will surely reap if you don't lose heart.

If there's anyone who understands about not losing heart, it's a parent. It's difficult to feed and clothe somebody who doesn't care that you're feeding them. It's very difficult when those members of your own household end up being the ones the devil uses, and what makes it worse is that they let him. It's done to shake your confidence. He wants you to lose confidence in the ability God has placed inside of you.

When the enemy comes at you, he comes at you hard and shows no mercy. He is determined to break you down. He is your enemy, and knows that without permission he can't really touch you. God has not given him access to defeat you without your permission. He has put a hedge of protection around you. He said that no weapon formed against you will prosper. He said, "I created the blacksmith who makes weaponry" (Isaiah 54:16). So he's saying "I have not given him permission to make a weapon that can defeat you, who I also created." The blacksmith does not have the ability to create a weapon that can ultimately take you out. The enemy's job is to deceive you and cause you to believe that he *can* defeat you.

Remember what we said about the boxer that suffers a mental blow and ends up believing the other person has the ability to knock him out because he had been knocked down before. Boxers are normally sure of themselves, making them by nature self-confident. So when they suffer a mental defeat, they lose it and are never the same again. You see this in sports all the time where both sides engage in trash-talk in an attempt to get into their opponent's head. They are trying to mentally wear their opponent out so they end up losing their confidence in their abilities. It becomes a war of words in an attempt to try to knock your opponent off by causing them to expend all of their mental strength. This is the enemy's strategy against us.

DON'T THROW AWAY YOUR CONFIDENCE

This is why the Bible says we are to cast down every imagination that exalts itself against the knowledge of God (II Corinthians 10:5). What is the knowledge of God? The knowledge of God is that you cannot be defeated! You have been guaranteed victory. You are the head and not the tail. You are above only and not beneath. You will be blessed coming in and blessed going out. Greater is He that is in you than he that is in the world. You are more than a conqueror. This is all about building your confidence up in the things of God. Why? Because God has promised to back us up and fulfill his word.

The boxer that loses his confidence is no longer as devastating as he used to be. When your enemy sees a flaw in your armor, he starts coming after it. Most boxers with undefeated records have it partly because they were able to intimidate their opponent. Once they see that that person can be knocked out, they lose whatever fear they had of that person's abilities and have more confidence in themselves. That's why God has allowed you to encounter some victories. If the enemy did nothing but win against you every time, you wouldn't think you could ever win.

Remember, confidence is a belief in either your own abilities or that of someone else. If you were confident in God's ability to do whatever he needs to do in your life, you would not hesitate to do what he told you to do. I am a tither because I am confident that God is going to make a way. If I weren't, I would not give. If I weren't confident that the chair would hold me up I would not sit in it.

Remember those early days when you were first exposed to the anointing, or to the Holy Ghost. Those were hard times when you first were introduced to salvation. In Hebrews 10, Paul is speaking to people under persecution because of their salvation. Some days it was you, other days it was your friends ... when we first got saved we had friends and family members that we encouraged when they began experiencing difficult times. "Hold on. God's going to make a way," we said. We were "Super Christians" and felt like we had all the faith in the world. Part of that feeling was a result of our newfound confidence in God, and that now that we're Christians we're not going to have any more problems. We had not yet read the scriptures that dealt with trials, tribulations and suffering. Nobody told you that suffering was a part of salvation. Somebody told you about the "Santa Claus" Jesus that was here just to bless you. You thought that by getting saved and hiding from the world, you were delivered from all the issues in this world, until you went back to the world and realized that was a lie.

If your friends were in prison, you stuck by them. If your enemy seized your goods, you let them go with a smile (meaning that you had mercy and grace), knowing they couldn't touch your real treasure. What is your real treasure, your salvation. The crown of glory that we will receive, those are heavenly treasures. That comes with your salvation. My treasure is not figurative crowns in heaven. It's that I am saved and going to heaven. And the Bible says that where a man's heart is, there his treasure will be also. I've seen many people who say that they're saved for real, but they slip away so easily... with one wink they're out the door. That lets me know that their treasure wasn't real. If your treasure were real you would lock it up. Anything you value that you don't want anyone to steal, you work to protect it.

Your real treasure is not your shoes, your DVD player in your car, or anything material. In our world today people have lost their lives because they stepped on somebody's shoe. The shoe was determined to be more valuable than the human life. People have more confidence in material things that are going to fade away than they do in human life and things that really matter. Christians can't turn around and be like the world and place more value in their own life than they do in their own salvation.

Now these are the things that cause us to suffer a setback and set us off, causing us to forget our real treasure. We all forget. That's why we have to live a life of repentance where at the end of the day we come back to God and ask him to help us again.

I've come too far to throw it all away now. I refuse to throw away all that God is doing for me over the fickle-mindedness of others. And when these situations happen, you have got to know how to turn your lemons into lemonade. Start making plans for the extra room. You've got to be more optimistic than pessimistic. Find the best in everything. My point is I'm not going to let that pull me off and set me back. I am staying focused on what God called me to do.

"I don't know what to do now that they've left me." Well, you need to stop your crying and put your confidence back in God. "I am going to kill myself." Do you mean to tell me that you value their life more than you value your own? God made you. That other person did not make you. You need to find out who you really are.

So don't throw it all away. You were sure of yourselves then... in the beginning... with all of those hard times and with all that was going on. The difference is that you have matured. Paul said *"When I was a child, I thought as a child. But when I became a man I put away childish things"* (I Corinthians 13:11). So the point is this, you've matured, in age but you must mature spiritually, so that you're stronger now than you were then.

Whatever you felt when you first got saved, it's still real now. You are to work out your own salvation with fear and trembling. God gives you that responsibility. We're all human. You can't let character flaws be an excuse for remaining wounded. We have to learn to grow from our experiences. You're always having to deal with somebody's personality, but don't let that hinder your relationship with the Lord.

You need to stick it out. Stay with God's plan so you'll be there for the promised completion. **Don't throw away your confidence, it will be richly rewarded.** You need to persevere so that after doing the will of God, you will receive the promise. Don't you understand that's what the enemy was after? In the beginning, God blessed you so that you would know he was good and to keep you close to Him. Babies are treated differently than mature sons. What Paul is saying here is that in this stage of your development you have to fulfill your end of the agreement in order to get to God's end for you. You have to do your part. After you have done God's will, then you will receive. **There are over 400 promises in the Bible**, so which promise will you receive? Whatever he promised you! But you don't get them just because you showed up. The Bible says after you had done his will, then you will receive.

What is the will of God for my life? What have you heard in your Bible study? Work out your own salvation, pray, fast, go to church, don't fail to assemble yourself among the saints, live a consecrated life, live a lifestyle of repentance, do good to your fellow man, feed the poor, clothe the homeless, find shelter for them, and do the best you can to be a good Christian. The will of God is all of that and everything else. Don't throw away your confidence. Don't faint. Don't quit. Don't give up.

I realize that may seem like a lot to do, but it's no more than what you do on a daily basis. It's a lot for you to get up and get yourself together to go anywhere, but you've mastered it. With headaches, stomachaches and kids acting crazy...you've mastered it. You've mastered getting up and doing what you don't want to do in order to get the reward. Dealing with supervisors, co-workers, the bad economy, setbacks, and layoffs...despite all of the stuff you have to deal with, you still get up every day, square your shoulders back, and go to work. You learn how to function in it. Well, you need to learn how to function in the Kingdom the same way. You can't let the world's system out-do God's system.

<u>After</u> you've done the will of God, you will eventually receive what he (God) has promised. "But you don't understand. I've been waiting on God, and I don't have it. He hasn't given me what he's said he would yet." Well, you keep quitting. I know you can repent, and I know God will forgive you for quitting, but in order to receive the promise you've got to start from the beginning and fulfill the will of God. You might have been here a long time, but if you keep quitting you've lost your seniority and your tenure.

DON'T THROW AWAY YOUR CONFIDENCE

But thank God that he's given you a second chance. If I gave you a test and you cheated on it then I'm not giving you the same test again. If I'm giving you a second chance to take a test, then I'm switching the questions. You should be grateful for the second chance instead of getting mad at me for changing the test.

Think back on those early days when you first saw the light. Do you remember how hard it was? Those were really difficult times. We have a tendency to look back on the past and only remember the good times, but the truth is the things you are going through now are not as hard as what you went through during the early days. During that time you were kicked around in public and found yourself the target of every kind of abuse.

You are stronger than you realize. You are an overcomer! I'm at a place in my life where I appreciate what I've been through. My wife and family know this to be true: I don't go home at night worried about my issues, whether it be good or bad. Why would I do that when I'm mature enough to know that God is in control? You have to understand you are in a spiritual war. If you continue to put your confidence in the flesh of people, men and women, mother, father, brother, sister, son, or whomever, you will constantly be setting yourself up for heartaches. It never shocks me who the enemy chooses to use as a distraction. So the word of God is here to encourage you, so you will not be discouraged. Your perception of life's challenges can cause you to live a little bit better or a little bit worse. So, perception is the key.

Scripture says, "don't be weary while doing good, for in due season you shall receive if you do not lose heart." When you're in the receiving mode, the enemy wants you to lose heart because he can't steal anything but your joy because if God blesses you, the enemy can't touch it. Whenever someone is being blessed there is something in their life trying to discourage them from enjoying the blessing.

Sometimes when people feel overwhelmed they lose their appetite and the flesh is discouraged from feeding itself. In the Bible, when David finished mourning the death of his child, the prophet admonished him "get up, wash your face and go eat." In other words, get back to where you need to be by feeding and nourishing yourself. Anything sick doesn't want to eat. When people get extremely sick they lose their desire for nourishment to where even the digestive system rejects food. Anything sick rejects food, so I don't let anybody feed me anything that's going to make me sick and cause me to reject God's people. I have to remain confident in God. I have to stay confident that he is going to reward me. I can't get caught up with an evil thought regarding someone I fed that doesn't want me to feed them. If you get caught up with that kind of thinking you will go on to become bitter and angry. You will be messed up and end up losing your focus, forgetting that you're doing this for God. God wants you to be thirsty for Him, not for people's approval.

Psalm 3:1 LORD, how many are my foes! How many rise up against me! When David was betrayed by his son and chief advisers, after they chased him out of the Kingdom he found himself in the wilderness and ended up singing, "Lord, I thirst for You." When you are seeking for the approval of people, you are thirsting for the wrong thing. God wants you to thirst for him. And if this ends up causing the people closest to you to chase you out of the kingdom you built in order for you to get to the heavenly place where he wants you to be, so be it. Some of us wouldn't be worshipping God today if it had not been for us being placed between a rock and a hard place. Some of us wouldn't be in church today if we hadn't faced some hard times that nobody could pull us out of... but God.

Now that we know who he is, why are we waiting until we get chased again? Why not do what we're going to end up doing anyway?

It's interesting that the scripture says, "don't THROW away your confidence." In other words, "you know who God is, and just because you're facing something that is new to you does not mean that God is new to you". You know that God is still faithful, and his mercies are new to you every morning.

This is why it's so important not to get caught up in other people's theories and opinions. You really cannot care about what people say or think about you. You will never get anyplace in God or be worth anything if you can't learn to stomach the things that celebrities stomach. Think about how many people want fame, despite knowing it means they're going to be in the tabloids, talked and lied about and everything else. Christians can be so sensitive over something as simple as a choice. "I like this music, but I don't like yours." The artist recording the music realizes that not everybody is going to like his music, but he still has to sing it. It's hard sometimes for ministers to hear people say, "I like that person's preaching better than yours." The root of this sensitivity is the spirit called pride, which happens when we become so caught up about what people think about us that we become unconcerned about what God thinks about us. I am more concerned about what God has to say about me than what the fickle minded person says.

When you've really been in the presence of the Lord you know how to let stuff go and no longer hold grudges. God starts dealing with you. If you're going to be given the full measure of where God is calling you to, you have to learn to let stuff go. If I were to think back on the things people did to me five or ten years ago and allow myself to get stuck there, I would still be stuck where they are now. The same people that were raising hell five years ago are still raising hell now. But I'm free.

Everybody knows somebody, whether friend or family, that keeps raising hell over and over again. Nothing has changed, but you should have. Imagine if you got stuck in a rut on the road and stayed on it? What would have happened to you? You wouldn't be prospering or going anywhere. Can you see that the enemy sees where you are now and was trying to stop it from happening? You might not think much of where you are now, but the enemy does, and recognizes that your faith and perseverance brought you this far. Because the enemy believes there is a God... he believes and trembles. The Bible says he believes in and fears God. So when God speaks something to you about your condition or outcome, or where you are going, the enemy stands up and takes notice. He asks, "How can I stop them?" The word says no weapon that is formed against us will prosper. You need to believe that.

Nothing they did bothers you. Nothing will be able to set you back.

God said you're going to go further. The enemy's job is to stop God's plan and direction in your life. When God says go two steps, the enemy says go back four. Why does he say four? The enemy not only wants to take you back to where you started, he wants to counter what God said. So, rather than give in to your flesh, you have to do what God says. If you ignore your flesh, if it's going to benefit God you must do what God is calling you to do. No matter what people think, you have to know what God says.

"But Pastor, how could I know everything that God is saying?" You don't, but the Bible says if you're filled with the Spirit of God He will give you remembrance. So all you have to do is have a sincere desire and intent to do the will of God then God will give you remembrance, and you'll begin to utter those things and perform those actions.

Nothing bothered you. Nothing set you back. So don't throw it all away now. You were as sure of yourself as you were then; it's still a sure thing. But you need to stick it out. Stay with God's plan, because there's going to be a promise of completion.

Sometimes we forget. Things can happen, and we freak out, and think just because something happened to us that means it changed God. But the Bible says he doesn't change. He's the same yesterday, today, and forever. God doesn't change. So stick to what God has planned for you.

The reason some of us don't know what God has planned for us is that we're too busy worrying about what's going on with someone else. We need to spend time with God in order to hear from Him regarding what he wants for our own lives, instead of

DON'T THROW AWAY YOUR CONFIDENCE

being so worried about what Brother So-and-So is doing. Stick to the plan God has for you.

"It won't be long now; He's on the way. He'll show up most any minute now, but anyone who is right with me will earn my loyal trust. If he cuts and runs, I won't be very happy. But we're not quitters who lose out. Oh no! We'll stay with it and survive trusting all the way." (Hebrews 10:37-39)

God is trying to teach you endurance. Don't you want to have endurance? You really don't know how much you've grown in God until something challenges your growth. You don't know how good you are on the practice field until you face somebody in a real game who challenges your abilities. The Christian has to be better equipped for challenges than the athlete. We need corrective criticism and discipline in order to excel. Armchair quarterbacks might be good in theory, but I'd rather listen to somebody who has a proven track record of success on the field... someone who's been hit a couple of times. Armchair quarterbacks or fantasy league football players might be good at picking the winners, but I'd rather have someone coaching me who has real world experience... Who can tell me how it feels to prophesy, get hit, and still have to prophesy and not ease my own opinion into it. Somebody who knows how to preach, get hit, and still have to come back preaching. Be an evangelist that even if he gets robbed still goes back and evangelizes some more. Be a missionary that has to deal with witches and still goes back. The apostle that goes to places where they hate you and you still set up a church. Be a teacher where nobody likes what we teach, and yet you still keep teaching until the glory of God comes down and everybody gets delivered anyhow. You'll never know how it effective you are in the Kingdom if you don't face adversity when it comes.

"For you have been my hope, Oh Sovereign Lord, my confidence since my youth." Begin knowing how to stay confident in the things of God. The Bible says to have no confidence in the flesh. But if I have confidence in my belief in God, in my belief in what I have witnessed God do, than the enemy can't knock me off my square. Remember what David said? "I've been young, and I've been old, and never have I seen the righteous forsaken, nor their seed begging bread." What he is saying is "I have experienced God in my youth, and I've experienced God in my old age, and never have I seen the righteous forsaken or in their seed (for generations) begging bread. I've watched those who are in right standing with God face adversity and saw God show up. He said he'd never seen them forsaken... forsaken means you were in need of God's help and it never came. It didn't say the righteous wouldn't need God's help. It says, "I've never seen the righteous be in need of God in not get what they need from God." And not only them, but also their seed. That lets you know that blessings are from generation to generation. This is bigger than you." (Psalm 71)

DON'T THROW AWAY YOUR CONFIDENCE

Proverbs 3:26 says, "for the Lord will be your confidence, and will keep your foot from being ensnared." God will keep you from being caught up.

Everybody is valuable because everybody is a soul. The Bible is saying don't lose your confidence. You started off in confidence, you knew God was real, and then the old life crept back in. The honeymoon is over. All of a sudden you think your salvation is not working. You want to fall back on your old habits and old things. All of a sudden you find out not everybody who calls himself a Christian lives holy. When Sally Sue tries to steal your man IN CHURCH... and Brother Bubba likes all the ladies IN CHURCH... and the choir messed up behind the scenes, but they sounded good when they come out... you are shocked to find out that some churches are just putting on a show... and you wonder why you lose your confidence. You cannot put confidence in the flesh. The truth sets us free. We must put our confidence in God and not throw it away.

Things are going to happen... but how are you going to deal with it? How you deal with it is going to determine what your outcome is going to be.

"So do not throw away your confidence, it will be richly rewarded." (Hebrews 10:35-36)

I was ministering to somebody the other day and told them, "I forgive you, but you don't realize what you did. Don't worry about me. You've got to worry about spiritual things now. All I can do is pray for you. I've got to keep my mouth shut because I don't want to say anything to fuel what's coming... it's on you now."

I'm cool because no matter what I've got to face, I'm still going to be richly rewarded. No matter what I have to face, whether it be sickness and death, plague or disease, homelessness or famine, in the end I'm still going to be richly rewarded. As you're growing and learning the things of God and how to live like a Christian, God will give you grace, and help you to trust him until your confidence in him is stronger and more developed.

Verse 36 says, "You need to persevere." Why do I need to persevere? "So that when you have done the will of God, you can receive the promise." What did God promise to you? You have to remember that the same degree of the promise also brings on a corresponding degree of persecution. Think about the NBA... playoff time is harder than regular season games. Why, because they're all champions. They've even adapted a slogan: "play hard or go home." That regular-season game won't cut it in the playoffs. The playoffs are where the best of the best are all vying for the title, so the trials are harder. Each challenge gets harder as the prize gets closer. As you progress and win each series, you face an opponent equal to your skill. It's the same way in the Kingdom of God. As you progress regarding the things of God you must also face and overcome the principalities that are set up to oppose you. And that principality has confidence that they're going to beat you. Now this is where your swagger comes in, Where you say, "you may have beaten them...you may have beaten my Mama, but you're not going to beat me! You may have beat my brother, but you're not going to beat me! You might have beat the others, But you're not going to touch this!" You have to have a confidence before you enter the battle that you're going to come out on top. You have to have that confidence in Christ because he told you, "greater is He that is in me than he that is in the world."

Do you really believe what you read in the word or are you just reading? Have you ever started to read a book and it started out good, then halfway through the book you forgot what you read and you found yourself just turning pages? Well, you can't do that with the word of God. The Holy Ghost will help you to remember. It's like having a book on tape: he just reads it to you.

You need to persevere so that when you have done the will of God You can receive the promise. You're not going to get God's promise if you don't do his will. Just "being saved" doesn't automatically give you the promise by default. The promise of God doesn't "kick in" after 90 days. You must do the will of God in order to receive it. Hebrews 11 is full of people who persevered and didn't lose their confidence.

Galatians tells us to "be not weary." The word "faint" means to lose enthusiasm or lose heart. When people faint in the natural world, they lose their strength and cannot stand. The Bible says regarding the man that faints in the day of adversity that his strength, or his faith, is small. Rev. Martin Luther King Jr. said: "The measure of the man is not what he does in times of peace, but what he does in times of adversity." In other words, what are you being tried and pressed on that you can still give glory to God for?

Stop waiting for people to write you a good eulogy. Some people get so bent out of shape over what their enemies are going to say about them. Don't give your haters a second thought. They're not worth your time. You need to use whatever you can to stir yourself up and keep focused on doing the will of God and not become distracted. Because at the end, you want to get what God has promised you. If you're going to be a Christian until Jesus comes back, you're going to have to learn how to live this thing for real. Learn how to live within the confines of what God has called you to be so you can receive your godly reward.

Don't throw away your confidence.

Chapter 2

Spiritual Warriors for God

"Now I, Paul, myself am pleading with you by the meekness and gentleness of Christ—who in presence am lowly among you, but being absent am bold toward you. But I beg you that when I am present I may not be bold with that confidence by which I intend to be bold against some, who think of us as if we walked according to the flesh. For though we walk in the flesh, we do not war according to the flesh. For the weapons of our warfare are not carnal but mighty in God for pulling down strongholds, casting down arguments and every high thing that exalts itself against the knowledge of God, bringing every thought into captivity to the obedience of Christ, and being ready to punish all disobedience when your obedience is fulfilled." (2 Corinthians 10:1-6 Amplified Bible)

When God calls you to be a spiritual warrior, you are never off duty. Ephesians 6 tells you to put on the whole armor of God. The spiritual war is always taking place. The word of God is admonishing you to always be ready to punish all disobedience after your obedience is fulfilled. *"Now I, Paul, myself am pleading with you by the meekness and gentleness of Christ, who in presence am lowly among you, but being absent am *bold toward you."* What Paul is saying here is that he has a certain type of boldness. He is telling them that "although there are times when I'm with you and don't really have much to say, **please don't misconstrue my meekness for weakness. I am always bold in Christ**. But I beg you to realize that when I end up meeting all of you face to face, I may not be bold with that confidence by which I intend to be bold against some who think of us as if we walked according to the flesh."

A lot of times you find yourself in trouble with spiritual authorities because you get confused and get in your flesh. A lot of times you get comfortable and casual, forgetting that you are dealing with spiritual authority. You must not forget who you are, and more importantly do not forget who your leaders are. The same authority they walk in when you like them is the same authority they walk in when you get an attitude. It does not change.

"For though we walk in the flesh, we do not war according to the flesh. For the weapons of our warfare are not carnal, but mighty in God for pulling down strongholds."

The weapons of our walk with God are mighty, not just when we are preaching or are on display. These weapons are given to us to pull down the strongholds we all face. Sometimes you think because you are anointed and come to church that you don't have any strongholds in your life. You get so comfortable sitting at the table with your leaders, holding their hands and walking with them and dealing with them in day-to-day activities that you forget they are in your life to pull down the strongholds that shouldn't be there. In case you forget this, they don't. They still have a job to do. For though we walk in the flesh, we don't war according to the flesh.

"For the weapons of our warfare..." Paul was talking about himself as well as the other apostles, and leaders. He wasn't talking about the sheep.

"Now I, Paul, myself am pleading with you by the meekness and gentleness of Christ, who in presence am lowly among you, but being absent am bold toward you. (He's talking about me to you, leader to student.) You can't start taking things personal just because you get uncomfortable. You don't attend a church just to be the pastor's friend. You go to the church were God sends you because you believe by doing so you can be better prepared for heaven by submitting to the authority there.

He says, *"I beg you that when I am present I may not be bold with that confidence by which I intend to be bold against some who think of us as if we walked according to the flesh."* He says, for all of you that have gotten carnal and have things in common with us, I'm going to be bold. He says, I am trying to be meek, but you don't know how to separate the man from the anointing. Often people don't know how to separate the two. When the leader has to be bold, it is with the best intentions for the believer. As a spiritual leader, you end up seeing all kinds of things in the body.

"For though we walk in the flesh, we don't war according to the flesh." He is talking about spiritual leaders in spiritual authority. You have to be careful which commentaries you are reading as well as their interpretation of what the word says. I'm not interpreting anything, I'm just reading you what's in the scripture.

"For the weapons of our warfare, (those of us in spiritual authority)..." This is not intended for everybody in the church because not everybody has spiritual authority or is walking right. Churches are a mixed multitude and not every Christian is spiritually mature enough to handle the authority they could walk in.

"For the weapons of our warfare are not carnal, but mighty in God for pulling down strongholds." We have the spiritual weapons to pull down strongholds. What are strongholds? What is it in your life that's keeping you from Christ? Whatever it is that is keeping you from fulfilling your true destiny in Christ is a stronghold. A stronghold in your life could be your personality flaw. You could be a person that has a great memory, and recite and memorize many things, but if you don't open up a book and read it, you're not going to be of any use to

anybody on that subject matter. So your deliverance may need to be more focused, more disciplined, more dependable etc.

The Bible says that little foxes destroy the vine. I see people all the time that let little things like being undependable render them ineffective in the Kingdom of God. They love God, but not enough to be dependable. You say you've given up everything, but you haven't given up that particular weakness.

The reason why some of us get into trouble is because we do stuff that is against what the Bible says. Just because you're unaware of the scripture doesn't mean your leadership doesn't have to deal with you on it. That is your shepherd's job. It is our job as spiritual authorities to "enlighten" and "encourage" when you say something that doesn't line up with the scriptures, or if you exhibit a behavior that does not line up with your calling.

"Every kind of thing, and every argument that chooses to exalt itself against the knowledge of God." The mind of God is the knowledge of God, which is the word of God. God's word is God's will, so if it doesn't line up with the word, it has to get shot down. For example, I was in court one time, and the judge was familiar with who I was because I knew someone he knew, and because of who I was in the community. Because of this, the judge prefaced all of his statements by saying "I have to rule based on the facts. Nothing personal." During a recess he came to

me and we had a chance to talk in the hallway, but then he issued a judgment that was favorable to me. Based on the facts, he had to do what he had to do. It's like that with police officers and anybody else who has the authority or responsibility to uphold the law. When they don't do that, they are abusing their power. They are being neglectful and are incompetent.

If you don't have integrity you can't function in the kingdom regardless of your qualifications in the natural realm. There are plenty of people that are gifted and talented, but inside they are morally corrupt. They know this Bible forward and backward, but what they're trying to do is piece it together in order to find loopholes so they can remain in their sin and avoid giving up their "alternative lifestyle." They say, "I ought to be able to live my life how I want to live, and God loves me anyway." Yes, God loves you, but he's not going to condone mess. Even when we are wrong and our conduct does not please God, we must remain confidant that His grace is sufficient. There are people out there that are morally corrupt, and when you rebuke them they want to quit on you and run. God's not going to support and uphold what you're doing if you're wrong.

So the spiritual authority in your life brings correction and direction, which leads you to truth and freedom. There was a woman and a man of prominence who got in trouble recently. When confronted, they were filled with pride, and were nasty to people in the press. The Bible says that pride comes before destruction and a haughty spirit before a fall. So they challenged the press to prove the allegations brought against them. They were prideful, and became haughty and arrogant in their sin. "We did it, so what, prove it!" Well, they did! The press pursued the story, found evidence of corruption and now they're going to jail. God bless them, I hope they repented, but it should have never gotten there. Sometimes the best thing to happen to a person is to be humbled. The only reason I am talking about this is to draw a parallel between their behaviors and how we act sometimes, thinking that we're going to get by living in sin and never get caught. **Sin is a major contributor to feelings of depression and therefore, a lack of confidence.**

Try the spirit by the Spirit.

I told my wife a long time ago that if a man hits on her and she says, "you can't hit on me, I am married," then she gave him grace by telling him she's in a committed relationship. But after she told him, if he does it again then he's disrespecting her. He's calling you an adulteress because even after you've told him you're in a covenant relationship, he continued to hit on you, which says, "all I want from you... because I cannot commit to you, and I cannot marry you, is sex." All he's saying is "there's only one thing you can offer me, and I don't care what your morals are." Would a person who knows what you represent disrespect you in such a way? If she's confident as a married woman, she's not flattered at unwanted advances. Likewise, I'm secure within my marriage. As a spiritual leader I have to be confident within my relationship. How often have we entered into bad relationships because of a lack of self-esteem? When God is in your decision-making, you're going to be all right. I'm not saying it's easy, but God will see you through it. As spiritual leaders we've learned the importance of encouraging one another. The enemy looks for any opening that he can find to come in, and discouragement and poor self-esteem are cracks in the foundation of a believer's soul. Your leaders are there to fight for you and encourage you.

"Casting down arguments and every high thing that exalts itself against the knowledge of God." What's the knowledge of God? His word. *"Bringing every thought into captivity to the obedience of Christ."* Every thought. We have the spiritual authority to bring every thought... not only our thoughts, but your thoughts also into captivity to the obedience of Christ.

So we capture them. We are to arrest them, subdue them, and make them obey the law the way it's supposed to be. Whatever your system was, once it's been captured and subdued, it has to change into the system God wants it to be. Paul said "I, Paul, a prisoner..." not to the world, but to Christ. If I'm in chains in man's prison, I'm still going to submit to Christ. If I'm in the chains in man's prison, I'm going to adhere to God's system.

"Now I, Paul, myself am pleading with you by the meekness and gentleness of Christ, who in presence am lowly among you, but being absent am bold toward you... But I beg you that when I am present I may not be bold with that confidence by which I intend to be bold against some who think of us as if we walked according to the flesh;" Bold to those who are saying they are just flesh and blood like we are. We can't be common with them.

If the man of God asks you to give in the offering, and you say that you will give if you can. You've lost confidence in what giving can do. Why? Because you've been abused, you've been mistreated, you've been tricked by other people. But when you submit to the leadership that God brings to you, and you want to treat them like they are the ones that abused you, it is to your own detriment. How can you fully get the benefits of being in the place of proper spiritual authority when you haven't fully submitted?

Maybe you're not impressed with how richly blessed you are. Maybe you think there's some tricks up the sleeves of your leaders, but once you understand that we do what we do by the favor and power of God, then you will realize that by submitting to it, it will be available to you in that very same way. It is a shared power to those who fully submit. If you're not impressed by what your spiritual leadership has as far as God's blessing and their accomplishments in God, then why do you stay? If you cannot recognize the blessing of being where God has sent you, you will never live in the full benefit of it.

For example, one Sunday I was ministering in my church and the Lord gave me a word to share to the congregation that debts were going to be canceled and the people who owed us money would be paying it back. In less than three weeks this is exactly what happened, not only for me, but for other members in the congregation who believed that word. The people in the congregation that didn't pay attention and recognize the word didn't receive that benefit. When the blessing comes, it is not only to benefit the leadership, but also those who submitted to the leadership. You have to trust your spiritual authority.

"Bringing every thought into captivity to the obedience of Christ." What does obedience mean? The word implies an attentive hearing, to listen with compliant submission. Compliant means that you're willing to go along with it. Submission means not doing what you're told to because you want to do it; submission is saying, "I don't understand. I might not even want to do it, but because you said to do it, I must and I will."

Now, I am a person in spiritual authority but those who work closely with me know that I am also submitted to authorities, and I am obedient to their authority to the letter. Some people might call it extreme, but it's reasonable. I can't tell my congregation to do something I'm not willing to do myself. When I say "go" to the people who have submitted themselves to me, I expect them to go. Well, if I am not a hypocrite then when I'm told to "go" by my spiritual authority I must also go. That type of submission makes you a very valuable and sought out person. It opens doors of favor to you like nothing else. People recognize the integrity you have by submitting to authority, and they respect that. When you've willingly submitted to that degree, you leave an indelible impression upon the people you come into contact with. People recognize and respect your authority because they see you respect authority by your submission. Ministries will seek you out because the authority you walk in enables them to do that which they cannot do. To be able to say, with boldness, what they cannot say. Don't you want to get to a place where you know you can speak a thing and it comes to pass? It has everything to do with fully submitting.

Not halfway, half-hearted submitting. As a leader I'm going to stay on my people and work them into a discipline so they can be what they're supposed to be in Christ, because the ultimate goal is for God to be pleased with your service at the end of your journey. You want to hear him say, "Well done thou Good and Faithful Servant." If I tried to compromise and become friends with the people that have come to me for leadership then, number one, I am providing them a disservice and second, I'm not doing my job as the spiritual leader. I'm not going to mess up my assignment. I'd rather take my time and cultivate a congregation consisting of people with integrity who are walking in their calling, and know how to submit to authority so they can walk in authority themselves.

Obedience signifies attentive hearing, to listen with compliant submission and agreement. Whatever you tell me to do I ought to do it, as long as it lines up with the word of God. That is the key. Don't let anybody tell you to do something that is not in the Bible. The minute they say something that's not in the Bible, run! You have to be wise, and you have to know the word. Don't let anybody fool you.

The word obedience refers to obedience in general, obedience to God's commands. Whatever God has commanded you to do, your leader ought to be able to bring that forth and you ought to be able to comply.

"And being ready to punish all disobedience once your obedience is fulfilled. Do you look at things according to the outward appearance? If anyone is convinced in himself that he is Christ's, let him again consider this in himself, that just as he is Christ's, even so we are Christ's. For even if I should boast somewhat more about our authority, which the Lord gave us for edification and not for your destruction, I shall not be ashamed." 2 Corinthians 10:6-8

DON'T THROW AWAY YOUR CONFIDENCE

The mindset of Paul is that he's bringing this to us for edification and not for destruction. I'm not saying this to hurt you; I'm saying this to make you better. You, being spiritual beings, being Christians and carrying the Spirit of Christ to a degree, we don't pull out belts to whip you, for the weapons of our warfare are not carnal, but all words will whip you, and bring correction.

He goes on to say, *"even if I should boast somewhat more about our authority which the Lord gave us for edification."* That means you could be rebuked and disciplined and it would be edifying. Isaiah said it pleased God the Father to bruise Christ. Whom the Lord loves, he chastens. You understand that is edifying? Anytime God brings a correction that causes you not to be destroyed that is edification; whether you like it or not. That couple I referred to earlier who are going to jail, I think it's the best thing to happen to them because they sought pastoral counseling...the pastor was with them in court. Submission is a place of safety.

We're coming to a season where people are going to seek out the truth. They're going to seek out leaders of integrity to submit to because it will be so rare. People have told me not to preach a hard word because people don't want to hear it since it exposes their sin. I believe that to a certain extent, but I believe that times are changing and there is shifting. People want to hear the truth.

"When the spirit of your leader rises against you, leave not thy post for yielding pacifieth great offense." Ecclesiastes 10:4

The Bible says don't leave your post. Start living that life. *You have to cultivate that strength and integrity inside of you.*

I believe in facing my fears. I believe in dressing for the job that I want, not the job that I have. I believe in giving to the fullest. I don't hesitate, I don't delay, I don't make excuses, and I have no tolerance for fear. I reverence and fear God only. That's it. You ought to be more fearful of God than anything else you are facing. You receive your power to overcome when you fear God. All power is in his hands.

Spiritual authority in any given church goes much further when it's understood by the people in that church. Jesus said a prophet is without honor in his hometown. If your perception of your leaders is all wrong, you will never gain the advantage that comes from having them as your leaders. When Jesus came into town all they saw was a carpenter's son. They didn't recognize him for who he really was and ended up missing it. Well, I refuse to miss it. I'm going to recognize the spiritual authority He has put over me, and I'm going to walk in the spiritual authority God has given me, and I want to see it benefit the people who follow me. I know it works; I'm living in it. The favor of God follows this ministry because of the leaders, and I want to see all my people walking in that favor. I will be favored by God because of my faithfulness and my willingness to submit.

J. Richard Evans Sr.

Chapter 3

Casting Down Strongholds

"Now I, Paul, myself am pleading with you by the meekness and gentleness of Christ—who in presence am lowly among you, but being absent am bold toward you. But I beg you that when I am present I may not be bold with that confidence by which I intend to be bold against some, who think of us as if we walked according to the flesh." (2 Corinthians 10:1-2)

A lot of people think what Paul is saying when he wrote to the Corinthian Christians was bold and cocky, but when he was up close and in person, he was scared. That is not what happened at all. Some people hold off from telling you what is really on their mind because they don't want to hurt your feelings; but if you pushed them into a corner they will tell you what they really think about you. It is not easy being bold, and it is even harder when you are in leadership. You really don't want people to tell you what they really think. I know I don't want God telling me what he really thinks about me. I probably wouldn't be able to come back from that. I just want enough grace that he'll keep on working on me because when God tells you what he thinks, that's it. He says the thoughts He has towards us are good and not evil. So we pray that he is just gracious in what he has to say.

"I entreat you when I do come [to you] that I may not [be driven to such] boldness as I intend to show toward those few who suspect us of acting according to the flesh [on the low level of worldly motives and as if invested with only human powers]. (2 Corinthians 10:5)

Paul is saying just because I am walking among you don't make the mistake of thinking that we're really on the same level. God has set some things up, and that's just the way that it is.

"For though we walk (live) in the flesh, we are not carrying on our warfare according to the flesh and using mere human weapons. For the weapons of our warfare are not physical [weapons of flesh and blood], but they are mighty before God for the overthrow and destruction of strongholds..." (2 Corinthians 10:3-4)

What's interesting is that everybody we come in contact with that has Kingdom authority has a different personality from another person, and not everybody is going to deal with things the same way.

You hear all kinds of things when you're in the ministry. I talk to my elders all the time, some church members think they don't need leadership because they're spiritual and can handle their own stuff. But then they cannot maintain any level of success and when defeat comes, all of a sudden the church has to pray for them. But when you were doing well, you were spiritual enough to handle your own stuff. I'm just saying it's no different than the people in the Bible who didn't respect their leaders' level of authority until they were in trouble and then they realized it's not easy to walk in any kind of level of success.

24 "Therefore whoever hears these sayings of Mine, and does them, I will liken him to a wise man who built his house on the rock: 25 and the rain descended, the floods came, and the winds blew and beat on that house; and it did not fall, for it was founded on the rock.

26 "But everyone who hears these sayings of Mine, and does not do them, will be like a foolish man who built his house on the sand: 27 and the rain descended, the floods came, and the winds blew and beat on that house; and it fell. And great was its fall." Matthew 7:24-27 (NKJV)

You'll be hard-pressed to find any kind of failure in my life that has lasted a long time. Have I experienced failure? Yes! However, I believe that the potential to fail is part of pursuing your goals. As you mature in the things of God, you get over trying to prove yourself to people. It puts you in a place where you don't fight foolishness. You don't fight foolish people, you don't fight people who make foolish statements, allow your lifestyle to speak for itself. There will always be those that will try to reduce you to their level. There will always be those that will try to minimize your accomplishments. There will always be those that will try to disavow your level of commitment to God. There will always be those that don't think you have the anointing to back up your success. There will always be those kinds of people. What you want is the power of God in your life to such a degree that **it speaks for itself**.

As a spiritual warrior, I am never off duty. I want the people in this vineyard to have a like mind, to have the ability or desire to follow the pattern being set before them so they will have accomplishments in their lives. Don't you want to achieve goals? Don't you want to look at an eviction notice and tell it to go away, and then watch it leave? Don't you want to look at a repossession and tell it to go away, and it does? Wouldn't you like to look at hunger and tell it to go way, and it does? Wouldn't you like to look at loneliness and tell it to go way, and it departs?

It is a biblical truth that if you rebuke the devil, he will flee from you. A lot of times for the Christian, he comes in the guise of these things: loneliness, hunger, desperation, poverty, sickness, illness, disease, dependence, etc.; whatever it is, it comes in those types of disguises, and ignorance destroys more than you think.

DON'T THROW AWAY YOUR CONFIDENCE

Ignorance is not bliss. Ignorance is the absence of knowhow, or knowledge. The Bible says, "My people are destroyed for a lack of knowledge." You do not want to live in destruction. You do not want to live a defeated lifestyle because you don't know. And wisdom is the principal thing.

I grew up in an environment of alcoholics, so I learned early how to deal with depression and more importantly, how to overcome it. I didn't like dealing with the alcoholic side of my family members. I would rather have had them sober. When you live with alcoholics as family members you learn how to both hate and love them at the same time. You want to embrace the sober person and reject the alcoholic. In my case, when family members were sober they were more conservative and guarded, but when they were inebriated they were affectionate. As a result of this, whenever I saw somebody with their arms open I learned to reject them. When you grow up in a house like that, where although there is love, there is also that divide, you learn how to live with rejection and end up living a life of rejecting people.

Now I've been delivered. The way I protect myself now is by not allowing people to sow discord around me. If I feel like you're about to dish it out on somebody and it's going to make me mad, I will tell you, "I don't even want to hear it." That's my way of keeping myself from hearing things that would make me want to reject somebody by avoiding hearing something I can't handle. God says he hates people that sow discord, so I try to keep myself away from those types of devices. What I've found is that your personality as a leader is both a virtue and vice.

Be not deceived: evil communications corrupt good manners. 1 Corinthians 15:33

My point is, in dealing with the people of God you learn how to deal with different personalities. You learn how to handle folks that may not be able to handle you. You learn how to handle people that might mishandle you, and you learn how to love people that will reject you. It kind of prepares you for the road ahead.

When you learn the things of God and don't try to live by your own understanding, God begins to deal with you in such a way that He can get glory out of your life.

As a biblical teacher, understand that I am very much aware of the fact that God is concerned with me living right. So I can't just come and teach you; I have to live this myself. I don't want to become one of these teachers, one of these ministers, one of these people of authority where the Word is always good for everybody else, but doesn't apply to them. I never want to be that kind of a person because, believe it or not, it is a miserable existence living outside of God's will. What keeps me on the straight and narrow to some degree is that I don't want to lose favor with God because I know what it feels like to be rejected. **I know what it feels like to love somebody that pushes you away.** I know what it feels like to hold your arms out to somebody who, even though they love you, won't embrace you because they don't know how to love. I don't want God to deal with me like that because I'm a sinner. It takes me back to those times when no embracing was there unless the person was inebriated.

So that means if you're not right with God, even though he loves you, there is no embracing because he has no fellowship with darkness. So even though he loves all of us, even the sinner, he says I'm not going to have fellowship with you if you are in sin. So it comes to a place where I am continually striving to have a relationship with God where when I speak to him He speaks back. When I'm in His presence, he likes me to be there. He's not trying to hurry and get out because of the stench of sin on some of my life. My point is to let you know that it is important for you to have a knowledge of God.

Whatever I need to know, the Bible says I should go to the elders. The elders have got to be sober, they have got to know what they are talking about, and they have to possess self-control.

For example, this scripture says, "casting down every imagination and every high thing that exalts itself against the knowledge of God." Let me tell you how powerful this statement is: God forbid, a woman gets pregnant and then comes to a spiritual authority. She says, "I am pregnant, I don't want the child" and the leader says, "You cannot get an abortion. That's against God". Now that is cut and dry, isn't it? After that, the woman comes to you and now says she is pregnant and you sympathize with her. You, being a spiritual leader become more involved because you see where she's coming from and have the compassion of God. Yet, because you are a morally correct person, a biblically correct person, you still say, "You're going to have to deal with that because God does not approve of abortion." God forbid if it was somebody close to you. God forbid if it was your child. In these cases it gets a little bit more involved and a little bit harder to be so direct. So, **you have to begin a pattern of binding and casting down** all kinds of things and bring your mind into subjection to the way God wants you to do things. The reason why some of us in this world cannot carry a level of success for long periods of time is because of a flawed moral character. I want you to be successful.

So what am I saying? Well, if you have a bad attitude, you can't keep a job. Or if you're not faithful, they will fire you. All this has to do with not having the right disciplines in your life to be successful. You see celebrities going through this all the time... you see a celebrity woman going through another divorce and no matter how beautiful she is, you wonder what's wrong with her that she cant stay married. She's going through her fourth or fifth divorce, (we're not even talking about the dates)... and you can't help but wonder what's wrong with her that she can't keep a man. She's got money, she's got success, she looks good, but nobody wants her for long periods of time. None of her relationships go past five years. She is the common denominator and has some inner issues that need to be addressed. What is it in your life that needs to get corrected; yet you're still trying to avoid it and live like you did before you got here? Especially when you come to a place of restoration? That means, "I came in broken, so whatever happens to me here is going to bring me back to a place of functionality." So even though you may have forgotten that you came broken, the leadership has not forgotten. If you go to a podiatrist don't get angry when he looks at your feet. That's what he does. That's his specialty.

So if God has you here, there are going to be issues that need to be dealt with. There will be issues that we discuss that are your issues, to bring you to a place of construction, and then completion.

Paul is dealing with the issue here, he's saying and I beseech you, I beg you...he is saying, "I need you to understand what I'm saying. I need you to get this so that you can be successful."

NOW I myself, Paul, beseech you, by the gentleness and consideration of Christ [Himself...

He is saying, "I am trying to appeal to you the best way I can."

The Message Bible translates it this way:

"And now a personal but most urgent matter; I write in the gentle but firm spirit of Christ. I hear that I'm being painted as cringing and wishy-washy when I'm with you, but harsh and demanding when at a safe distance writing letters. Please don't force me to take a hard line when I'm present with you."

You see, Paul is really our hard-line, bottom-line person. He is asking what you are bringing to the table. He is saying, if you force me to be a hard-line, bottom-line person you're going to come up short.

The Bible says when it comes to business, to be men, but you still have to have the Spirit of Christ. Paul was saying "don't force my hand." he is saying if you force my hand, I'm going to be bottom-line. That same anointing that can discern this and discern that, speaks into your life and can do some damage if it isn't controlled. And that will mess you up.

Paul says, *"Don't think that I'll hesitate a single minute to stand up to those who say I'm an unprincipled opportunist. Then they'll have to eat their words. The world is unprincipled. It's dog-eat-dog out there! The world doesn't fight fair. But we don't live or fight our battles that way, never have and never will. The tools of our trade aren't for marketing or manipulation, they are for demolishing the entire massively corrupt culture. We use our powerful God-tools for smashing warped philosophies, and tearing down barriers erected against the truth of God."*

Most of us put up the barriers because we're scared. Do not be afraid to succeed. We automatically go into self-destruct mode when we feel we're going to be challenged to succeed. Believe it or not, if you've lived and confronted and endured failure... once you have accepted defeat it's hard for you to be a champion anymore. Once you have been beaten down by the world, by relationships, by church, and somebody starts trying to challenge you, you think they're being hard on you when the truth of the matter is they're not pitying you. So you come to a place of restoration, and it's not that they don't care about you, their concern is not that you've been defeated, their concern is the fact that you are not living like a conqueror. We have all faced defeat. You have to know how to overcome it. So mindsets have to change.

You have to get deliverance from past church experiences. I'm not beating you up. I am firm but fair. As you read this I pray that you are being restored and healed in your soul.

It's a tough world out here, and we want you to be successful wherever you go in life.

The tools of our trade aren't for marketing or manipulation, but they are for demolishing that entire massively corrupt culture. We use our powerful God-tools for smashing warped philosophies, tearing down barriers erected against the truth of God, fitting every loose thought and emotion and impulse into the structure of life shaped by Christ. 2 Corinthians 10:5

A lot of times your success is on the way, and you're afraid. I know a guy who bought a lottery ticket. He visualized all that he was going to do with the winnings then when the drawing came he refused to look at the ticket. He said, "If I look at the ticket and I haven't won then reality sets in and all that I envisioned goes away." So why buy the ticket?

The thought of being able to win was enough to build him up. But the fear of finding out that he lost was enough to keep him from finding out the truth. He never looked at the ticket until it had already expired. One day he was watching the news and they were talking about how the person who won the lottery never showed up and claimed the prize. That's when he decided to go look and discovered that he had won, but he was a day late. He never looked at the ticket because he never believed he was going to win. Wouldn't that make you sick?

But you know what's going to make you even sicker? When you get to heaven thinking you had failed, only to learn that victory was right there but you stepped over it. Victory was right there but you never opened the door. Victory was right there, but you left the church too soon. Victory was right around the corner but you wouldn't turn the corner. Victory was on the other end of the phone but you wouldn't answer it. As God is my witness, I know when I stand before God, there are going to be some areas that He will bring clarity to me that I missed.

So why do you have leaders? Why do you have spiritual authority if you're not going to listen to them? What's the purpose of your going to church if you're not going to take anything you've learned and do something with it? What's the purpose of going? This is the barrier.

A man once said to me, "It is a terrible thing to meet someone who can't read. But it is an even greater travesty when you find someone who can read but never opens the pages of the book and dares to do so." Who's the worse off? The one who couldn't, or the one who wouldn't? I think the person that could but wouldn't is worse off than the one who didn't have the ability.

So what barriers are in front of you that YOU need to overcome to be successful? The Bible says these barriers are erected against the truth of God. So someone with an anointing in their life will come by to tear them down. **We've come to tear down everything that chooses to exalt itself against the knowledge of God**. So the anointing is more than jumping and shouting and grabbing ears. My goal is that when all the music stops, you have some power so that when you finish reading, you can speak to a situation and see it change, knowing you have resurrection power. When you finish reading this book, is there anything added to your life that makes you more of a Christian than when you began reading? You say you have scripture, but what good is it to you if you never use it?

Most police officers go an entire year without ever pulling their gun out of their holsters; and most go through their entire career without ever firing a shot. But you can't be a Christian who never uses any of the scriptures God gave you, and when the enemy came at you, you just let him get you. You died with your gun still in the holster, fully loaded. That doesn't make sense to me. Why do it? I didn't get saved to be miserable. I grew up on hard times and food stamps. That's rough enough. I'm sorry; I don't feel closer to God on welfare. Not me. I just don't. That's a lot to have to be praying through…soup kitchens and all that. I've been in the Good fellow box. I knew the box when it came. I don't care how you wrapped it; I knew what it was. My kids don't know it like I knew it. They didn't hit the rough patch I hit. Try sliding cheese under your pillow and getting woke up because the mice beat you to it.

I told my wife I loved my mother because during all of that time, I didn't even know we were poor. We were fed, clean, and she cared for us the best she could with what she had. The house was kept clean (and it still is). I watched her and how she tackled things and decided, **"whatever barriers that are in front of me, I'm going to break them down."**

My mind would get to wondering, "How can you work one job for your whole life and not get bored?" Now, I know I'm normal because the average person changes careers two to three times during their lifetime. So don't think if you're in your second or third career it means something's wrong with you, because it's rare for someone to just work one job forever. But my mind would get to wondering to the point that when I thought about it, I'd shake my head, "No! I can't do it." I couldn't comprehend working the same job for the rest of my life where I was any more than I could comprehend "borrowing sugar." I hated borrowing sugar. Really, I hate borrowing anything. You'll notice that if you borrow anything from me I say "keep it." I don't want you to owe me, because I don't like falling out with people over borrowed things, so if I know I need it back, I'm not giving it to you. If I can't afford to give it to you, I don't loan it. That's me. You have to have a good credit rating with me. If you have a good credit rating with me and I loan you something, I really, really trust you. Or I trust you and can afford to give it to you. So, before it gets to a point where it's a problem, I'd rather just say, "You can have it."

So backing up... My mind couldn't comprehend certain things, so I began to confront stuff. Any barrier I confronted, whatever the obstacle was, I told myself "I'm not sleeping until I conquer this thing." If you bought me a toy, I wanted to know how it works. You can ask my mother. If you bought me a toy that ran by remote control it's not going to work tomorrow because I was opening it up. Anything electronic – I wanted to know what made it tick. The absence of knowing what made it tick was a barrier. I'm the same way today.

Any barrier that we have to confront, we have to know that the anointing comes to give you power, to empower you to pull it down. That's why boxers have a coach. You can be in the fight whooping on somebody, and the coach still tells you, "You know if you'll do it more this way, you can just take them out." Or if you're losing, your coach tells you, "This is why you're losing... you're not using enough of your jab..." or whatever. This book is my way of coaching you. It's not to fight the fight for you. That's why so many people are getting in trouble; they are trying to get the pastor involved in their fight.

"...tearing down barriers erected against the truth of God..."

Whatever barrier the anointing comes to tear down was erected against God's truth, so the only thing that can tear it down is the anointing. It didn't just say that our tools tear down any erected barriers. It says they are to tear down barriers erected for the specific purpose of keeping you from the knowledge and the truth of God. When people talk about their imaginations, philosophies and their gibberish, it's a barrier constructed, developed, and erected with the express purpose of keeping you from the truth of God.

What is the truth?

"I am come that they might have life, and that they might have it more abundantly." (John 10:10)

That is one of the truths. You can piece it in however you want. So if God wants you to live and live well, there's going to be some obstacle that has been constructed to keep you from living well. All the things that you have been encountering – all the things you've been through this week, this month, or this year were designed to keep you from success in God.

Whenever the enemy starts fighting you like he's been fighting you, you'd better know you're on the right track. For example, when our country was at war in Afghanistan and Iraq, it would have been foolish to go to Mississippi and say you were fighting in the war. That's not where the battlefield is. So if you're in Mississippi and talking about how hard the battle is, everyone knows you're lying. But the closer you get to Iraq, the more you understand the reality of the war. We're talking heavy artillery, we know where the stronghold is, and there is a real enemy that we are aware of. So when you're there, don't think the reports of war are strange. Don't forget that you are in a war.

"But Pastor, you don't know what I've been going through..." As a general, I EXPECT to hear we're going through difficult times if we're at war. Remember, David didn't get in trouble until he came off the battlefield. Some of you are built for this. I was sharing with the elders that the emphasis we minister on regarding certain topics in the church is different than other churches in another demographic. It's still the truth of God's word, but some congregations need a different level of a certain ministry because of what they're walking through and have to confront in their own life. It takes a Creflo Dollar type of minister to show people who have money how to manage it. That's part of his anointing. People who cannot relate to that aspect of his ministry want to denounce his whole ministry. That would be like me speaking to a group of Marines and end up talking about the Navy. Stay in your lane. You let the Marines do their thing, let the Navy do its thing, and let the Army do its thing. Stop attacking people in other branches of the military or other branches of the Body.

So, all that I've encountered this year has been because barriers were constructed to keep me from being successful in Christ.

So what do you do? Let's go back to the text:

"...tearing down barriers erected against the truth of God, fitting every loose thought and emotion and impulse into the structure of life shaped by Christ."

The anointing that comes to smash warped philosophies, and tear down barriers also comes to fit every loose thought and emotion and impulse into the structure of life shaped by Christ. So the same anointing functions in more ways than one. So for every wild or loose thought, for every wild or loose emotion, for every wild or loose impulse, there is an anointing that comes to bring order to it.

Think about that. Especially when you're used to being independent and you've been surviving. "Fight or Flight," depending on your natural instinct. Then, someone comes along and says, "You're too wild. Let's get some structure." Going back to the boxing illustration, it's like the difference between a sub-par fighter and a boxer. The one just likes to fight or brawl. There's really no structure to it. The other has more finesse and strategy. You might not like his style because there's not a lot of action involved, but at the end of the round he's the one that's accumulated the most points. The fighter might have looked like they were doing a lot, but his hits weren't effective even though his arms were flailing. To the crowd it looked like he was doing well, but to the judge he didn't get any points. He really didn't do anything to win the round. So the coach says, "Don't be wild, you'll get knocked out. You can't be wild against this guy, because he isn't panicking. You're swinging all over the place, and he's waiting for you to swing and miss, or he's trying to tire you out." It's like being in a war against someone who really doesn't have the strength to fight – their goal is to use your own weapons against you.

You have to have a strategy, so God will send someone with an anointing who will say, "You've been flailing. You've been all over the place. You don't have a strategy, and the enemy is just waiting for you to get tired." The minute you get tired – I don't care how strong you are, how gifted you are, how skilled you are – the minute you get tired, and the enemy has enough stamina, you're done.

Remember, your weapons aren't carnal. Don't try to come at me in a carnal way. Paul says, "I'm a wise master builder." So you're coming from the mindset of someone who has been through what you're going through. Been there, done that. I'm no stranger to the flesh. I've persecuted and killed Christians. I'm educated." Paul is saying, "I've seen it all. I've come out of a bloody empire. I'm a Roman citizen. I am not naïve."

How often could we have been successful had we not been flailing? Flailing is a sign of naivety and immaturity. What does flailing look like in a Christian's life? Praying double-minded, going to everybody's church, collecting philosophies from everywhere...and you wonder why you haven't gained any ground. All you've gotten was tired.

Don't you know that's a spiritual attack? The enemy's tactic is to confuse you until you're so messed up that even though you're not "sinning," you'll never make it. And then you don't want to listen to instruction, you don't want anyone telling you what to do, and you have no structure. You don't realize that when you take that position, the enemy is still winning. He still wins, because God wants you to have a good life on your way to heaven, but you're miserable. On top of that, you can't win souls because nobody wants what you've got. So the enemy renders you ineffective.

"...fitting every loose thought and emotion and impulse into the structure of life shaped by Christ."

Your thinking can't be all over the place, and your emotions can't be all over the place if you want to be successful. You have to stop acting on impulse. The anointing comes to stop you from being so impulsive, or acting without thinking. Retail stores and grocery stores strategically place their products in an attempt to try to make you buy impulsively; from where they position the bubble gum and magazines at the checkout to the music they play in the mall.

So the anointing comes to tear down warped philosophies...

What does it mean to be warped? Warped is when something can appear straight, but it's actually on a curve. For example, when you're playing pool, if you don't realize your cue is warped you think you're shooting a straight shot and you don't understand why it's veering to the side.

A philosophy can look and sound right but still be warped. So if your philosophy is warped, it takes an anointing to come in and straighten it out. Because you won't know it's warped without having the truth to compare it against. You don't know your cue is warped until you roll it on your pool table and see it wobble. You have to measure it against a sure standard. You might try to play it off by saying, "It's still a cue stick." But play against someone who's good, and you'll see how that warped stick defeats you. If you're going to win you need everything lined up in your favor. You can't afford to be handicapped in any way. A good pool player examines all the aspects of the game before he starts. They check the cues, the pockets, if it is a 6-foot or an 8-foot table – and they adjust their execution accordingly. The anointing does the same thing. It examines the terrain or atmosphere and takes them into consideration before devising the strategy.

So when people who are used to acting on impulse get around an anointing, they feel constricted because the anointing restricts them from flailing out on impulse. You can't just move out like you used to. Impulsive people are usually wishy-washy or double minded. One day they're going to be a sanctified, single Christian, and the next day they want marriage. One day I'm chaste, the next I'm in need of companionship. They're impulsive – and the anointing breaks that yoke. How can you be trusted with ministry if you're so easily swayed by impulse? If you haven't been delivered, you're dangerous.

When the anointing comes to break that, how do you respond? Are you emotional and find yourself wanting to cry all the time? Are you easily offended? Moody? You must learn how to walk in love by forgiveness, while allowing your spirit and soul to make the necessary adjustments. We're training people to work for God. The anointing comes to you and points out what's wrong that needs to be corrected. If you get offended with that you won't change, and you won't be successful. You'll be stuck.

If you listen to coaches and trainers talking to fighters in their corner, they're always telling them something to convince them to do better. If they feel they're not getting through to them they'll say, "Listen, if you're not going to fight, I'm going to throw in the towel for you!" If you keep coming to the pastor with your issues but you're not willing to change, he really can't help you. The way of the transgressor is hard. Your sin and disobedience will catch up with you. The anointing comes to confront the sin so that you can be successful. If you let sin stay, it's going to trip you up. The enemy is going to use it to trap and ensnare you. There was an evangelist who tells the story of how she was struggling one time, and the preacher sent a driver to take her home. She said she had to hurry up and run into her room in order to resist temptation. Now first of all, in my humble opinion, the preacher should have never sent a man alone to accompany her. He wasn't using wisdom in this situation. The evangelist said she knew this was the attack of the enemy, but she didn't fall for the trap. How many women would have succumbed to the snare?

  It's just like dealing with people in my former profession. I was an Optician by trade, and my wife and I owned our own business. I would come into contact with some famous people. I am a "ring-person," meaning that I believe if you're married, then wear your ring. I would see all these people coming into my store with little babies, but no rings on their fingers. These are people that are supposedly gospel entertainers, but when I saw that I questioned their integrity. In that scenario, they were either divorced with babies, which can happen to anyone, or they were never married to begin with. Either way, these are issues that were never confronted and torn down with the anointing.

The anointing comes because it wants you to live a life that has been shaped by God. The anointing comes to help you live a Christ-like life.

Continuing in our scripture:

"Our tools are ready at hand for clearing the ground of every obstruction and building lives of obedience into maturity."

When you hear someone addressing your immaturity, don't automatically become defensive thinking, "They're putting me down." No. It's part of growth. Fruit has to mature before it becomes ripe. Is that an insult? No. It simply means, "Until you're ready." The anointing comes to make you ready. Sometimes you can't see what it is that needs to be tweaked in your life because you're living it. That's why God brings people with an anointing who can come in and show you your blind side. Whether the flaw is brought to your attention or not, it's an issue and a barrier to you. But God wants you to have full disclosure so you can be successful. He didn't say it was going to be easy, but if you'll conform to the instruction you'll have victory.

God has a plan for your victory.

I was teasing my son the other day and I told him, you want to have all these things... Imagine God gives it all to you, and you can't get anybody with it. Imagine you've got the car, the money, and everything else you're asking for, but then God tells you "Go get married. Be responsible. Make a commitment and stick with it." You have to know why you want these things. We want and we want and we want, but we're not looking at the big picture. There's a girl in Vegas that went gambling after work and won a multi-million dollar jackpot but was injured in a car accident driving home and now she's paralyzed. All of her millions of dollars now have to be used to take care of her. Which do you think she'd rather have, all of that money or the ability to walk? To use another example, what good would it do for me to ask God to send me 5,000 members if I didn't have enough seats or restrooms to accommodate that number of people? Some of the things we're asking for, we're really not ready for. This is what the anointing is for.

"Our tools are ready at hand for clearing the ground of every obstruction and building lives of obedience into maturity."

DON'T THROW AWAY YOUR CONFIDENCE

What I believe we can have is what Paul said. What he's really saying is, "We can be a dream team," a body where each joint is supplying, and all the cylinders are clicking. That is my desire as a pastor. Every part comes together and is able to sustain itself. It's mature and it's sober with the right heart motives.

Remember when America first brought together the basketball "Dream Team" for the Olympics: they brought in the best of the NBA. They went in and won games almost without even trying. But you see what's happened since then: every nation they played had to step up their game in order to contend against them.

So what I'm saying is that when God blesses you like that, everybody has to step up his or her game. We can't take a day off. We're in the race to win. The anointing is here to let you know, "You've won before and you'll win again." You can't ride on last season's victories because your enemy has stepped up his game. You need to train harder and be more resilient to keep winning. You've got to up your game.

J. Richard Evans Sr.

Chapter 4

Spiritual Boot Camp

"Casting down imaginations, and every high thing that exalteth itself against the knowledge of God, and bringing into captivity every thought to the obedience of Christ." (2 Corinthians 10:5)

We've been talking about being in a spiritual war. A spiritual war requires spiritual warriors. While you're in preparation, the enemy is preparing as well. What you have to understand is that the enemy is so regimented that all he thinks about is how to bring you down. That's just his whole regiment. Day in and day out, he thinks about how to bring down the Christian.

I'm a movie buff. I get lost in the enjoyment and recreation of watching entertaining cinema. Has anybody seen the movie "The 300?" There's a scene where the king and his army of 300 men are marching. They meet up with another warring nation who have come to unite with them so they will have more soldiers for combat. An observation is made concerning the small number of only 300 soldiers, in comparison to what appears to be more from the neighboring army.

Upon closer analysis it is discovered that although the neighboring army appeared numerous, there were very few men with actual fighting experience. The question is asked what they do for a living? One says he was a blacksmith some were farmers; none of them were professional soldiers. However, the 300, which had significantly less in terms of number, when asked, "Spartans, what is your occupation?" made this loud noise like the Marines would when they shout "hoorah" that let you know that every last one of them were warriors. Even though outnumbered, your experience in warfare and survival makes you a warrior. A lot of times people think mere numbers will get the job done, when in fact it is not the numbers that make the difference, but the dedication.

7 Then the Lord said to Gideon, "By the three hundred men who lapped I will save you, and deliver the Midianites into your hand. Let all the other people go, every man to his place." **Judges 7:7** *(NKJV)*

That is seen in the Old Testament story of Gideon and his army where God reduced his army consisting of thirty-two thousand men to a mere 300 who had a desire to fight. These 300 men defeated an enemy so numerous that the Bible says they were like a horde of grasshoppers covering the land. Alexander the Great utterly defeated the mighty Persian Empire despite facing armies that outnumbered his forces ten to one. Additionally, the average age of his soldiers was 65, compared to a much younger Persian army. Many men of God have gone forth and done great things with less.

A lot of times you forget that your enemy has been doing his job for a very long time. With centuries of experience, he is very successful at bringing many Christians down. And so here you are praying, Lord, make me more skillful in warfare. Then once you start going through the training you can't get mad at God because if you want muscles you have got to lift weights. Lifting weights involves resistance. I'm lifting something heavier than me in the hopes that I'm going to be able to handle it better.

In other words, if I'm resisting the devil time and time again, even though I might get tired of doing it, what I have to realize is I'm building up muscles in areas that I never utilized before. The more I deal with, and the more I go through, the stronger I'm getting. I know you don't want to hear that; nobody wants to go through that.

There are some things that are good for you that you would not necessarily choose for yourself. The Bible says God tries no man, but life challenges you. And you're thinking that God has forsaken you, but he already promised that he would never leave you or forsake you.

So why am I going through what I'm going through? Could it be the result of answered prayer?

I am going through the process of dealing with the things that are going to make me stronger.

A few years ago I was attacked in my body, and as a result, was hospitalized. I prayed while I was laying up on the gurney, I felt death trying to take me. My enemy wanted to finish me. My wife says she recalls me telling the devil, "I'm not dying today. You might as well leave me alone. Because when I get my strength back I'm going to serve God more diligently than before."

Do you think for one moment when you're on your sick bed or when you're feeling defeated the enemy, the devil, won't bring you down, and that he's going to have compassion on you? If he feels he's got you now. He's going to try to finish you off.

The things that you're going through are the things that will build you up so you will not get yourself to a place of confusion where you doubt yourself and God's abilities.

Even the Apostle Paul found himself struggling with thorns in the flesh. The Bible records him saying, "I asked the Lord on three separate occasions to take the affliction that I was going through away from me. And he wouldn't do it." And the Lord told him "my grace is sufficient" (2 Corinthians 12:9).

⁹ And He said to me, "My grace is sufficient for you, for My strength is made perfect in weakness." Therefore most gladly I will rather boast in my infirmities, that the power of Christ may rest upon me. (NKJV) 2 Corinthians 12:9

When we are suffering and going through certain things, Christ is our confidence. He is our strength. Yes, you might be going through some tough times financially especially in this current economy, put your faith in the word of God. However, you have been trained and taught over the years on how you should be conducting yourself while going through these trials.

God is building you up in your faith, getting you to a place where you don't react to the things the way others do. No matter what you go through, you still have praise on your lips. No matter what the distraction is, you still know how to pray. No matter what the attack is, you don't panic because you've been trained for warfare.

My Father was a military man. My mother's oldest son and one of my older brothers were both military men. I have another brother who passed on a few years ago who was a MP in the Army. I wanted to be a military man, so before I was even old enough to join or enlist in the Army or the Marines, I was already studying it. The Marines are what I really wanted to go into. I learned how they operate, and I knew about basic training. I heard about live rounds being shot over your head so that when you get into a real firefight you don't panic, you don't freeze. I heard about all of the stories where people can get killed if they don't listen to their instructions or orders or if they freak out and panic. I knew about all of that and I wanted to be ready. I didn't know at the time that God was building me up to fight a different kind of war.

⁴ For the weapons of our warfare are not carnal but mighty in God for pulling down strongholds, *⁵ casting down arguments and every high thing that exalts itself against the knowledge of God, bringing every thought into captivity to the obedience of Christ, ⁶ and being ready to punish all disobedience when your obedience is fulfilled. (NKJV)* **2 Corinthians 10:4-6**

When my wife got pregnant with James, I was going to join the Marines.

There was a security officer at the place where I worked that said, "Man, if you join the Marines it might destroy your family." He said, "You are young, you're just getting started, it's going to take you away from your family. It's not good for your family." Despite my desire to be a Marine, I listened to that advice. I talked to a few other people who said the same thing and told me to just raise my family. Don't get me wrong, joining the Marines has been a great choice for many brave Americans, it just wasn't the correct choice for me at the time. I didn't know that God was going to send me in a different direction.

Here you are in basic training if you will, going through live rounds and everything else in order to prepare you for the time when it's not friendly fire; for the trials of life that are going to come your way. Don't let anybody tell you that when you become a Christian you instantly go from being Clark Kent to Superman and you're going to be able to outrun a locomotive, be faster than a speeding bullet and all the other stuff that goes with it. You're going to fly. As a matter of fact, it might bring you real low for a season. **But at some point in your Christian walk you're going to rise.** Yes you will. You're going to rise.

So my advice to you is to learn how to be you. Who did God call you to be? I tell husbands, wives, and parents this all the time. Don't you lose your marriage over your children who will eventually leave you to carry on with their own lives. The minute they get old enough they are going to leave you for whatever they think they are in love with or whatever they think they desire to do. It doesn't have anything to do with love. They are going to live their lives and you can't destroy your marriage, your covenant, for someone else. So you better learn how to live your life. You can love and raise them, but don't give up your life for theirs, because by nature children have been programmed to receive, grow and move on.

When we mature, it blesses us to give back, more than it does to receive.

When we learn to have an appreciation for being able to love while feeling rejected at times, we've matured. I've learned how to appreciate being a giver. I can commit to teaching you, and ministering to you, and feel rewarded. When I was stricken with illness a while ago, my concern was, "OK, is everything in place so that the people can get fed?" I still had my suits laid out for church. My plan was to go minister to the Lord's people. If they say I have to stay overnight, I'll just make the second service. My mind was set. I didn't panic, I didn't freak out. Why? Because there's always a plan in place for whatever the warfare is going to be.

What plans do you have in place? Are you excited about going to church? Are you still rejoicing in the things of God? You are training for reigning, and I'm rejoicing with you! So don't throw away your confidence.

"And lest I should be exalted above measure through the abundance of the revelations, there was given to me a thorn in the flesh, the messenger of Satan

to buffet me, lest I should be exalted above measure. For this thing I besought the Lord thrice, that it might depart from me. And he said unto me, My grace is sufficient for thee: for my strength is made perfect in weakness. Most gladly therefore will I rather glory in my infirmities, that the power of Christ may rest upon me. Therefore I take pleasure in infirmities, in reproaches, in necessities, in persecutions, in distresses for Christ's sake: for when I am weak, then am I strong." (2 Corinthians 12:7-10)

Some of you are stronger then you think. I might be getting up in age a little bit, but when I was laid up on that gurney I realized that even with 98% of my artery blocked I was still stronger than the people living outside of God. That's not meant to be an arrogant statement. It felt good knowing I was sustained because of my labor and the power of God, because faith without works is dead. I had to do something and it felt good to know, laying up there on that hospital bed that my labor wasn't in vain, and people came to see me, it was encouraging. My wife actually shocked me when she told me people were praying for me. I said "Wow," she said, "no, you don't understand, calls have been coming in from around the country." I said, "Wow." That was wonderful and I'm very appreciative and overwhelmed.

When you've been wounded, and at times, abandoned, you learn to survive and make things happen seemingly on your own. However, when you realize that others care for you, it's comforting. You appreciate the prayers of the righteous. You learn how to believe in and trust God even more.

Are you doing it on your own? No. When you find out that everybody else is joining in and praying with you it makes you feel good. It's where you are. King David says he encouraged himself in the Lord. You can be in a room filled with faith, but if you allow yourself to feel defeated, you will miss your opportunity for breakthrough. "I learned how to encourage myself." So when you find out that somebody else will encourage you, it's a bonus. When you cannot find anybody to pray for you, you'll pray for yourself and then you find out other people are praying with you, it's the icing on the cake. *When you find out that even when you're not able to rejoice, somebody else's rejoicing for you is an added blessing.*

Don't you know that the struggles you are encountering are building you up to that place?

The struggles you face are building you up to that place where you start realizing that you don't have to build yourself up on false humility and tricks to keep moving forward. Once you know that the God you serve is with you and understand that; "Greater is He that is in me than he that's in the world", you can do all things through Christ who strengthens you. *You have something that God can work with - all of that is on the inside of you.*

DON'T THROW AWAY YOUR CONFIDENCE

There will be times when nobody is around to encourage you that you will need to search within yourself for strength. There is something working on the inside of you that can help you in your time of trouble. You are equipped to handle the wiles of the devil. Don't be afraid that the devil is going to come and mess with you. Some of you are quietly saying, "I don't need that, I don't need that hell." You are already going through hell. What do you think the devil is going to say? "Go ahead and say something. I'm going to mess with you tonight." He's already messing with you. Don't let him get in your head.

"For God hath not given us the spirit of fear; but of power, and of love, and of a sound mind." (2 Timothy 1:7)

"There is no fear in love; but perfect love casteth out fear: because fear hath torment. He that feareth is not made perfect in love." (1 John 4:18)

The Bible says God does not give you the spirit of fear because fear involves torment. Anytime you are at a place where you're afraid to exercise what you have learned about Christ, you're fearful. You have a spirit operating in you and it is taking shape. One moment it will show up as fear, the next it will show up as sickness. It will show up as confusion. It will show up as opposition, or disease. It's taking shape in you, but it's a spirit that does not belong in you. God doesn't want you to have a spirit of fear that involves torment. Think about that.

11 And they overcame him by the blood of the Lamb, and by the word of their testimony; and they loved not their lives unto the death. (KJV) **Rev 12:11**

I knew a guy years ago that listened to my radio program. He had brain surgery and cancer, and couldn't sleep one night. He listened to the radio program and afterwards slept peacefully for the first time in weeks, maybe months. As a result, he joined the church. But he went back to sinning and then that fear crept back on him. That brother was scared to give his testimony. He was scared to testify about what God had done. Fear had crept back in, but we knew he was drinking and trying to party and all kinds of things; He was trying to live a double life - and fear had crept back in. He was afraid to tell his testimony.

That's why I say don't throw away your confidence. I'm confident that I'm saved. Are you confident that you are healed? Are you confident that you're delivered? Are you confident that through Christ you can do anything? I mean for real. Don't say it if you're scared. Are you confident that out of the abundance of your heart the mouth speaks? Are you confident that life and death is in the power of the tongue?

DON'T THROW AWAY YOUR CONFIDENCE

"Pastor, I'm going through..." I know! You're in training, baby. God can trust you. Why you? Out of your entire family, why you? Out of all your co-workers, and all of your classmates, why you? A lot of times we ask, "why us" when it's bad. Although God has blessed me, I still go through my trials? I've watched people close to me die. I have my struggles. Don't you know this is all part of the enemy's plan? Let me see how much I can throw at him at one time, the devil says. Didn't I say you have got to learn who you are? If the enemy has been studying you, he knows you. Don't fool yourself, however, God knows you better.

Don't let anybody else know you better then you know yourself. You're in trouble. He's watching your pattern. A real enemy watches your pattern. Studies your pattern. Studies your route, and your little proclivities. The devil has got to get you down, because you're a real foe, a threat to the kingdom of hell. Therefore, don't be an easy target. If you lack discipline, no rhythm to survive, he can get you. But if you're a survivor, prayer warrior, praiser, a worshiper, then you're equipped for battle.

I'm trying to get you to a place of being confident hearing God's word as it pertains to you. Confident in the spirit of the word as it pertains to you. Confident in the vision that God has for you or the prophesied place that God wants to see you in, and one of those things is understanding who you are in Christ.

Paul knew who he was. He said I have a thorn in my flesh. I went to the Lord three times and he just told me that his grace was sufficient. What is Grace? Unmerited favor. In other words his grace is enough. It might not take the pain away but you can endure it. What does a pain pill do? It doesn't take the pain away, but it masks the pain. That's what it means when he says my grace is sufficient. Don't worry about it. You are going to be able to make it through this because of me. "Lord, it ain't gone away yet." Don't worry about it.

When we get a headache and take a pill to make the headache go away, we confess that the headache went away. We were making a wrong confession when we say that, the fact of the matter is we just don't feel the pain anymore. The headache is still there. But because you no longer feel the effects of it you say it went away. Shouldn't we be like that with the things that we are going through in life?

By faith I ought to be able to confess I'm not sick anymore. I believe I'm going to experience manifested healing, even though the evidence of the illness might still be there. By faith I have to believe that it's going to go away, and the grace of God will keep me in a place where I can't feel the effects. Trust me. I've seen it many times.

So the enemy's job is to come and tell you you're sick. Why are you acting like you're not? Your

DON'T THROW AWAY YOUR CONFIDENCE

job is to say by God, by his stripes, I'm healed. You have got to know you are healed. Have you ever noticed that the enemy always knows exactly what to say to break you down and which buttons to keep pushing? He knows you. Cover your buttons. Guard your heart. That's what the Bible says when it tells us to resist the devil and he shall flee: Put your hand over your buttons.

We'll confess in a minute, "I've got one last nerve and you're about to get on it." Instead, confess, "You aren't going to get on my nerves" isn't that the more positive confession?

"Death and life are in the power of the tongue: and they that love it shall eat the fruit thereof." (Proverbs 18:21)

I'm telling you not to throw your confidence in God away. Your confidence in God's ability to create in you what he needs you to be. The country is going through money problems but no one is jumping out of buildings like they did back during the Great Depression. When you live through some things you learn how to survive them. So you ought not to respond to them the same way. Nobody wants to go through some of the stuff that we have to go through. But again, we need to hope in God that we're coming out.

One of things I've said for years is "I might be going through, but I'm coming out" - that's a confession. Isn't it? Paul said the reason I think I'm enduring this thorn in my flesh is so I won't get a big head – that's what he said "lest I be exalted..." I'm laying hands on the sick, they are recovering. I'm performing miracles, and I'm doing all these wonderful things. So that's why I believe I'm carrying my thorn in the flesh. That's what Paul says.

What is it that you're going through that keeps you before the Lord? What is it that you are dealing with in your life that keeps you praying? Because we're human we tend to drift. Things get a little too good, and we don't pray like we used to. You have got to be really mature to do that - and even then if things aren't really "going on" your prayer gets a little stale. You know it by heart.

"Now I lay me down to sleep I pray the Lord my soul to keep," you know you've been saying that same prayer since your Mommy and Daddy taught you and here you are, big Momma yourself.

I caught myself doing this. I was in my twenties praying, "Now I lay me down to sleep..." I am not lying. I had been saved and everything, and finally I stopped myself and said "hey!" My Dad is dead and gone, I've got a family all my own and I'm still praying the same prayer "God bless Mama and Daddy." I had to stop! I had to break myself out of that routine and pray a different prayer. I had to learn to say, "Lord, bless my wife and my children and my mother." I had to change the pattern. How many of you still pray "...and God bless all my brothers and sisters, and my grandmamma and big momma and 'em..." and now here you are thirty-five with a different life and still praying the same prayer. Don't you know the enemy will figure that out? So you have to learn how to make some adjustments.

Paul says, "Concerning this thing I pleaded with the Lord three times that it might depart from me. And He said to me, 'My grace is sufficient for you...'" Grace in Greek is "charis" which comes from the same root word as "chairō" or "joy" or "to rejoice." It is the word for God's grace as extended to a sinful man. It signifies unmerited favor, undeserved blessing, a free gift.

So God is saying, "You can't earn this, you can't pay for this, and you can't buy it, but because I choose, I'm going to make sure that I bless you, I'm going to bless you so good that whatever you're dealing with, if you keep your eyes on me you will not feel the effect of what it's coming to do to you."

Remember, the enemy comes to do what? Kill, steal and destroy. But God says I come that you might have life..." So Paul says, "Whatever I've been afflicted with..." He says, "Whatever I'm going through, it's enough to bother me." No doubt it annoyed him, after all he was doing for the Lord, it frustrated him.

I had to minister to some of the saints not to be angry with God, thinking God had done something wrong because of what I went through. I said, "Wait a minute!" I understand your love for me, but please don't challenge God. We can't always explain why we face adversity. God gets the glory, but we never are to place blame, I said "no, no, no you got it wrong; my testimony needs to be upgraded" so God has to give me a testimony of how I can make it through. Your testimony gives you power.

So here, Paul is saying, "This affliction was bothering me so much I went to the Lord three times." This is a man of faith; this man knows God. He's seen him, been knocked off his beast by Him, blinded, and been through a lot of trials... He knows the laws of the Old Testament. He knows the text, knows the script, and knows the scroll. He's an educated man; so educated in fact that he had to be convinced that God was real. He was fully persuaded. Yet he has an issue that he takes back to God three times, and he didn't say in the same day. Yet the Lord had to say, "Listen Paul, my grace is sufficient. Whatever's going on I'm going to give you the ability to overcome it." But He didn't take it away.

A lot of us feel that overcoming something means it is no longer there. You just don't react. I'm an overcomer. Listen, I was born on the East side, and I grew up in the projects. I still believe that I'm an overcomer. Same dirt, same atmosphere, different perspective. You walk in the same dirt, you're living in the same atmosphere, but your attitude has changed. You feel like you've overcome it. Think about that. So don't stick your nose up too high. Same dirt, different day, do you hear me?

God is equipping you to be an overcomer. That's why you're learning to endure the hardships of life. God in His Sovereignty will cause you to suffer things that would blow your mind if he revealed them to you. Jesus picked twelve men to be His students, disciples, and followers, and yet one of them was a devil. Judas sat so close to Him that when He talked about one betraying Him and dipping his bread in the sop, nobody saw who dipped. When he got up they asked, "Where is Judas going? To pay alms?" Jesus relied on him to take care of the business of the ministry. Yet Jesus knew him enough to know that he was the one who would betray him. But he never freaked out, never tripped. Jesus knew who Judas was.

When Peter said that Jesus wasn't going to die on the cross, Jesus said "get thee behind me, Satan." Then he told Peter, when he saw the spirit that was in him, "Peter I hear all that you're saying, but before the cock crows three times you are going to deny me." Yet he didn't kick him out of the assembly and give him his walking papers. Instead he said, after you're converted... You're going to go through challenges; you're going to backslide, give up the ministry, you're going to give up everything, you're going to turn your back and walk away from me. You will deny me, you're going to do all of those things... but after your conversion, you're going to be able to come back and strengthen the brethren.

> ⁹ And He said to me, **"My grace is sufficient for you, for My strength is made perfect in weakness."** Therefore most gladly I will rather boast in my infirmities, that the power of Christ may rest upon me. ¹⁰ Therefore I take pleasure in infirmities, in reproaches, in needs, in persecutions, in distresses, for Christ's sake. For when I am weak, then I am strong.¹¹ I have become a fool in boasting;[a] you have compelled me. For I ought to have been commended by you; for in nothing was I behind the most eminent apostles, though I am nothing. (NKJV) **2 Cor. 12:9-11**

In other words, you're going to go through a whole lot but it's going to make you stronger. Why would Jesus send Peter to strengthen anybody if he was weak?

> ¹³ When Jesus came into the coasts of Caesarea Philippi, he asked his disciples, saying, Whom do men say that I the Son of man am?
>
> ¹⁴ And they said, Some say that thou art John the Baptist: some, Elias; and others, Jeremias, or one of the prophets.

DON'T THROW AWAY YOUR CONFIDENCE

¹⁵ He saith unto them, But whom say ye that I am?

¹⁶ And Simon Peter answered and said, Thou art the Christ, the Son of the living God.

¹⁷ And Jesus answered and said unto him, Blessed art thou, Simon Barjona: for flesh and blood hath not revealed it unto thee, but my Father which is in heaven.

¹⁸ And I say also unto thee, That thou art Peter, and upon this rock I will build my church; and the gates of hell shall not prevail against it.

¹⁹ And I will give unto thee the keys of the kingdom of heaven: and whatsoever thou shalt bind on earth shall be bound in heaven: and whatsoever thou shalt loose on earth shall be loosed in heaven.

²⁰ Then charged he his disciples that they should tell no man that he was Jesus the Christ. (KJV) Mat16:13-20

Jesus said, "upon this rock I will build my church and the gates of hell will not prevail against it." Don't you think that denying Jesus, turning from him, and cursing him were gates of Hell? Jesus said they won't prevail. So you would think that when Peter turned back from following Jesus for a season that the gates of hell prevailed. But the story wasn't over.

God is speaking to you. We hear prophecies but we must prepare for the process between revelation and manifestation. We all hear what we want to hear, not understanding the process that's going to get us there. *"I see you. You're going to lose twenty pounds..."* yeah, but nobody tells you how you're going to be tempted to eat that sandwich. Those twenty pounds aren't going to fall off on their own. "The Lord has spoken and we receive the word of truth, but those twenty pounds are going to disappear by you putting down that sandwich, putting the chips up, putting the ice cream away and exercising. After the stomach pains and aches, your twenty pounds come off and someone will look at you and say, "that prophet was right." But if you hadn't done your part the prophecy would still be lingering.

What are you going through? I want you to come out of this session with confidence in God's ability to do in you exactly what he said he was going to do.

"And he said unto me, My grace is sufficient for thee: for my strength is made perfect in weakness. Most gladly therefore will I rather glory in my infirmities, that the power of Christ may rest upon me." (2 Corinthians 12:9)

What's an infirmity? Sickness, disease, something that I'm going through in my flesh. Paul said I would rather glory in my infirmities or boast in my weakness, that the power of Christ may rest upon me.

You're anointed because of what you're going through. Most anointings are birthed through trials.

Some of you are going through the fire, but that's when God's anointing shows up. He said, "I rather glory in my infirmities, that the power of Christ may rest upon me." He says I boast in my infirmities that the power of Christ rests upon me.

So when I started going through, I started saying, "Thank you Jesus." Why do you think people do that? They know what's written in the Bible. When you know the word of God, you face adversity differently. When you get in some of those churches where the saints of God really know how to pray and praise God when they are going through, it's an encouragement. They know when they start going through hell to say, "I thank you Jesus. Thank you Lord. Hallelujah." They don't hang their head. I watched Apostle going through, and he praised God while he was going through, I was sitting there saying, **"Man, I want to be saved like that."**

Nowadays, we want the anointing for all the wrong reasons. Some just want to look good. We acquire the style of the preacher, but not the substance or study habits. As soon as we start going through, we faint.

¹⁰ *If* you faint in the day of adversity, Your strength *is* small. (NKJV) Proverbs 24:10

And it shall come to pass in that day, *that* his burden shall be taken away from off thy shoulder, and his yoke from off thy neck, and the yoke shall be destroyed because of the anointing. (KJV)Isaiah 10:27

I want the anointing that destroys yokes! As a babe in Christ I would watch the elders praising and thanking God. You'd think they were crazy. And you couldn't sit in their church too long. The power of God was in there to such an extent that everything they did would end up knocking you across the back of the head. You'd think that God was going to come down in the service and get you.

"And he said unto me, 'My grace is sufficient for thee: for my strength is made perfect in weakness.' Most gladly therefore will I rather glory in my infirmities, that the power of Christ may rest upon me. Therefore I take pleasure in infirmities, in reproaches, in necessities, in persecutions, in distresses for Christ's sake: for when I am weak, then am I strong. (2 Corinthians 12:9-10)

These infirmities he's boasting about are the

same ones he said he didn't want, but God refused to take them away in that season. He said I learned how to boast in them. "Yea, I'm walking but I'm going to be driving soon. Money might be a little tight, but I'm still eating. The doctor says I'm sick but I'm going to believe God's report that I'm healed." That's boasting, not saying, "I feel down, I feel sick..." not confessing it, but boasting in it.

Paul says, "therefore I take pleasure in infirmities..." In needs, in persecutions, in distresses for Christ's sake. "For when I am weak..." so who told you that you were weak? When I first made that statement, some said, "What is wrong with this man? Doesn't he understand what I am going through?" Some thought, "He's in denial. He just doesn't want us to know what he's dealing with. He's trying to get us to feel good, but we're going through unbelievable struggles. Why don't you just tell us, Pastor?" No. You become strong because of what you are going through. Read your Bible.

So I say, "don't throw away your confidence." That's not being arrogant, it's not being haughty it's not being high-minded. What Paul is saying is, "I know who I am in Christ. I'm a spiritual warrior. I'm never off duty. I'm supposed to go through challenges, and we're supposed to pray." You're supposed to fast. You're supposed to rally together.

⁵ casting down arguments and every high thing that exalts itself against the knowledge of God, bringing every thought into captivity to the obedience of Christ, (NKJV) 2 Cor. 10:5

I need to know who God is. How do I know who God is? I have got to know the word of God and the mind of Christ; I have to know the Bible. I must know God's will. What's God's will? His word.

Scripture says you have to cast down every imagination and high thing that exalts itself against what you know about God. But you can't cast anything down with any type of authority or power if you don't know what you're casting down. "I'm going to cast down this illness." You know what? What you need to be saying is, "Lord, I want to be healed and while I'm waiting I'm going to rejoice. By faith, I receive my healing."

How many of you come to church and have been fighting the same old thing and sometimes you drag yourselves in because you don't feel like your prayers have been effective. I know you're trying, but you're missing the fact that in your infirmity while you're waiting on God, His grace is sufficient. Praise God. While I'm waiting I'm still going to praise. While I'm believing for healing to come, I'm encouraged in the word.

"...And bring every thought into the captivity to

the obedience of Christ." The word obedience signifies attentive hearing. To listen with compliant submission, assent, agreement.

So I need to bring all that I'm going through to the obedience of Christ. What does God say about it? Not what the world says, not what I think.

⁵ Trust in the Lord with all your heart, and lean not on your own understanding; ⁶ in all your ways acknowledge Him, and He shall direct your paths. (NKJV) **Prov. 3:5-6**

We need a little bit of direction at times. Believe it or not, we don't know everything. Sometimes you have to say, "I've got to go pray about this." Take everything to God in prayer.

"And having in a readiness to revenge all disobedience, when your obedience is fulfilled. Do ye look on things after the outward appearance? if any man trust to himself that he is Christ's, let him of himself think this again, that, as he is Christ's, even so are we Christ's." (2 Corinthians 10:6-7)

And be ready to punish all disobedience when your obedience is fulfilled...So I'm not casting down anything with power until I've lined myself up with God and fulfilled my part of the equation. How am I going to be able to punish somebody else who goes against the word when I'm going against it too? He said your obedience has to be fulfilled. What is your obedience? I know how to react when I'm going through, so I can rebuke the devil because I'm not bound by him.

You can't swing at your enemy when you've got your hands tied.

I need to be able to respond to what's coming against me. This is the reality of Paul's authority:

"Do you look at things according to the outward appearance? If anyone is convinced in himself that he is Christ's, let him again consider this in himself, that just as he is Christ's, even so we are Christ's." (2 Corinthians 10:7)

I made a statement earlier; I said you've got to know who you are in Christ.

Don't think more highly of yourself then you ought to. Amen? It doesn't make a difference if everyone in the world is praying for you if you don't have enough faith for yourself. You need to know who you are in Christ.

The reality of Paul's authority:

"For even if I should boast somewhat more about our authority, which the Lord gave us for edification and not for your destruction, I shall not be

DON'T THROW AWAY YOUR CONFIDENCE

ashamed - lest I seem to terrify you by letters." (2 Corinthians 10:8-9)

Remember, I started off saying I'm not being prideful, arrogant, haughty or high minded, but this is a biblical principle. I'm not ashamed to say I know who I am in God. Never be ashamed to say who you are in God. I don't care what the enemy says through your friends or your family, "who do you think you are?" No, not who do I think I am, who do I know I am.

"...Lest I seem to terrify you by letters. 'For his letters,' they say, 'are weighty and powerful, but his bodily presence is weak, and his speech contemptible.' Let such a person consider this, that what we are in word by letters when we are absent, such we will also be in deed when we are present." (2 Corinthians 10:9-11)

You must know who you are. Don't wait until you're afar off. Stand your ground regardless to what people may say about you, know who you are. Have that Holy Ghost boldness. Confidence.

So don't throw away your confidence. You've got to up your game.

J. Richard Evans Sr.

Chapter 5

God Will Sustain You

"Cast your burden on the Lord, And He shall sustain you; He shall never permit the righteous to be moved." (Psalm 55:22)

God will sustain you. You guys are Christians and that means you are believers. Believers of what? Of this word - not just the gospel, but the entire Bible. When people give me a Bible I ask them if it has both the Old and New Testament in it - because that's the kind of guy I am. I believe the whole Bible. Somebody told me there were sixty-six books in there. I believe all of it.

I do not teach you principles that you can't find in the Bible. Everything that I teach, you will find in the Bible. The beauty of it is that I don't have to twist anything. I just give it to you like it's written. The Bible says that faith cometh by hearing, and hearing by the word of God. (Romans 10:17). I don't know what people do when they leave here on Sunday, but I've been taught that the people who grow are the people who show up for Bible study; the people who get taught the word of God. The Bible declares that if you are going to have any kind of faith, it will have to come by hearing the word of God being taught.

I can't just hear the word of God, I've got to apply it to my life. Because faith without works is dead. (James 2:26) That means you can read the word, but unless you apply it to your life you will be just as fruitless as somebody who doesn't.

The Bible says God has not given us the spirit of fear; but of power, and of love, and a sound mind, (2 Timothy 1:7). Then there is another scripture that says the reason he hasn't given you fear is because fear involves torment (1 John 4:18). You're not to be tormented by anything. Even though you see the signs of the times, you're not supposed to be afraid because fear is an indication that you don't trust God, and most people that are afraid are those that need to be delivered.

I teach that it makes no sense to me that we be so hypocritical and point out the sins of the lesbian, the homosexual, the whoremonger, the adulterer, the liar, the thief and the murderer - and here we are, AFRAID. It's all sin. Our job as Christians is to believe what God said. When I'm wavering in that belief, I need you who are spiritual, or more spiritual at the time, to help me to be restored.

When the spirit of fear comes on me, I need someone around me to say, "wait a minute, that isn't God." I need somebody to shake me back to myself and remind me of who I am in Christ. Sometimes you revert back to a babe because of babes or unbelievers coming back into your circle. Believers revert back to not believing when unbelievers have more influence, because spirits transfer. People don't follow titles; they follow influence.

I welcome non-believers to Church. If they have a bad spirit I'm not worried because I know we've got enough influence to take it on. That's why you can be a Pastor doing a great work and people will follow someone in the pews right on out the Church and into destruction because that person has more influence over them.

We see it all the time. I have commented about it on occasion. Even though you're a member of a church, your Pastor is the person that you follow. You can't fool me. I watch; that's my vantage point. I notice when certain people don't come to church others follow. They're following their influence. However, my concern is that the influence being followed is incapable of sustaining what it attracts.

Once I knew a girl that was leading the worship team, her spirit was all screwed up. She was foul, always offended. I told her she was in sin. Anytime someone said something to her she got offended. Even a "good morning" greeting would upset her. She was in sin, and she was scared. She feared criticism and the insecurity of her sins. Remember, fear involves torment.

We've been doing this for a long time. And we've done it without being fearful. I started with nothing, but through the guidance of the Holy Spirit have accomplished a few things. Opposition was there the entire time.

I remember when I first moved out of my Mother's house into an apartment. We had to buy everything. I had a little one-bedroom apartment; and I had to buy a broom, a mop and all the stuff that goes with it. I said "Lord they didn't tell me all this." I learned that there was a lot to purchase when starting off from scratch. I got over my fear of starting fresh, and along came people who helped me continue. God has placed great men and women of integrity in my life. I would have never made it without them. My spiritual parents always put the Lord first, and remind me to do the same.

26 *Put me in remembrance: let us plead together: declare thou, that thou mayest be justified. (KJV)* **Isaiah 43:26**

6 *But without faith it is impossible to please Him, for he who comes to God must believe that He is, and that He is a rewarder of those who diligently seek Him. (NKJV)* **Hebrews 11:6**

An example of your faith is when you go to God. The minute I go to God to remind him of what he said in His word, I'm exercising the fact that I believe Him.

DON'T THROW AWAY YOUR CONFIDENCE

If I'm putting him into remembrance, then I want him to reward me with the promise that he's made for my life. A good leader will never let his people starve. If there is a famine, he is going to look out to ensure his people are fed in the famine. The reason kings had loyal subjects is because they could feed and protect them. If they couldn't do that there would be a revolt. We serve a mighty God, and none of us are going to suffer long.

"*Cast your burden on the Lord, And He shall sustain you; He shall never permit the righteous to be moved.*" (Psalm 55:22)

Who are the righteous? What makes you righteous? The fact that you're in right standing with God and that Jesus is an intermediary between you and God. This is what makes me powerful now that I have an advocate with the Father. I don't have to suffer long.

[18] For I reckon that the sufferings of this present time are not worthy to be compared with the glory which shall be revealed in us.

[19] For the earnest expectation of the creature waiteth for the manifestation of the sons of God.

[20] For the creature was made subject to vanity, not willingly, but by reason of him who hath subjected the same in hope,

²¹ *Because the creature itself also shall be delivered from the bondage of corruption into the glorious liberty of the children of God.*

²² *For we know that the whole creation groaneth and travaileth in pain together until now.*

²³ *And not only they, but ourselves also, which have the firstfruits of the Spirit, even we ourselves groan within ourselves, waiting for the adoption, to wit, the redemption of our body. (KJV)* **Rom 8:18-23**

Our righteousness is as filthy rags, but we're still in the right place. Don't let the enemy make you think you're not worthy. You've been doing all this repenting. You've been fasting, consecrating, tithing and giving, don't allow the enemy run roughshod over your life? The devil is a liar. God will sustain you.

Sustain means to provide somebody with nourishment or the necessities of life. God will sustain you.

I have three questions for you.

- Are you a willing vessel? Are you willing to trust God?

"Restore to me the joy of your salvation and grant me a willing spirit, to sustain me." (Psalm 51:12 NIV)

DON'T THROW AWAY YOUR CONFIDENCE

A lot of people don't really have the willingness to trust God. They want to do it themselves. They're scared. I know that if God takes his hands off of me just for a moment, **I can't handle it. I don't have a safety net other than Jesus**. If I had finances in the bank and began to trust them, with the economy being the way that it is, could I really trust it?

What does the Bible say about trusting in finances more than God? The Bible says you aren't supposed to trust that. Instead you are supposed to trust in God. So what is God saying to us when we turn to him because what we were really trusting in was getting in his way? Is your money your God?

Don't get me wrong, I need some money. You all need some money.

19 A feast is made for laughter, And wine makes merry; But money answers everything. (NKJV) **Ecclesiastes 10:19**

I want everybody to have some money, but shouldn't God be our primary focus?

My point is that we don't want to be afraid. We want to be safe. I'm in a better community now and the first thing I did when I moved in was have them put a security system on the house. The installer said, out here, for what? I explained to him that I was born and raised in Detroit. In other words, my lifestyle conditioned me to such a degree that I took it with me even though I didn't need it. Some of you have alarm systems on your cars along with a club, just in case. Could it be there are things in you that are really not for your benefit, but because they make you feel safe you've placed them there?

So that first question was, are you a willing vessel? Are you willing to trust in God? Restore to me the joy of my salvation. What this means is that I need to be able to be happy in trusting God regardless of what is going on around me. Restore to me the joy of my salvation.

Am I a willing vessel? Yes, I'm a willing vessel and I'm mature enough to understand that I have to know enough to enjoy being saved, even when things are not going my way. So I cannot let life dictate to me how I'm going to live. "Well I was born like this, and I'm going to stay like this." The devil is a liar. I've been born again. I've got a second chance.

Are you convinced that God will help you?

Am I willing to trust God? In other words, don't confess that you're going to trust him just to find out when you need to, you won't. Don't just give it lip service. Let faith develop within you, so that when it's time to walk by faith, you have the ability.

6 But let him ask in faith, nothing wavering. For he that wavereth is like a wave of the sea driven with the wind and tossed. (KJV) **James 1:6**

DON'T THROW AWAY YOUR CONFIDENCE

We used to say, "don't sell no wolf tickets..." because God will find you out. Don't point your finger at others. Don't look down on people. Don't snub people. Focus on your faith level. Remember, but for the Grace of God, go I. Everyone has to deal with their own faith and development.

God has a trial tailor-made just for you. I know the Bible says that God tries no man. Life does a great job of doing that so we're going to say: life has a trial tailor-made just for me.

So am I convinced that God will help?

"Strangers are attacking me; ruthless men seek my life - men without regard for God. (Selah) Surely God is my help; the Lord is the one who sustains me." (Psalm 54:3-4)

Everything you have ultimately belongs to God. I've read that the sale of safes has skyrocketed because people who used to trust the banks said, "Oh my God, I've got to take my money out of the bank because these banks are folding left and right."

The federal government bailed the banks out in order to stem the people's panic when the banking industry was struggling. After receiving billions of taxpayer's money, do you know what the bank executives did? They went to Vegas for twelve, thirteen days. They're not thinking about you. They got that government money and then had the nerve to give each other bonuses. If I did that I'd be in jail. If I took government grants and went and put a driveway in at my house, man they'd have me in jail. They'd have me all over the news, reminding people that the money was given to me by the government. If it's like that, give me a couple of billion - I'll pay it back. I will, I'll pay it back in increments.

"Strangers are attacking me..." That means my adversaries are coming against me, right? "Ruthless men, to seek my life. Men without regard for God." So, I'm going through adversity – bill collectors don't care that I'm saved or not, they want their payment. Do the people coming after you for bills care if you're saved or not? I know you're all saying, "They're ruthless?" Yes. Everyone who wants me to pay them back is ruthless *(I'm being facetious).* That's how I'm looking at it right now. I'm not going to curse them or anything, but maybe I don't have it right now. If you call me again now you're harassing me. Call me five times now you're really harassing me. Seek my life right?

"Surely God is my help..." Where am I going to get it from God? How am I going do this? When I'm confronting my issue and have done everything I could do to correct it, but can't, what do I do?

Faith is not "I know how to do it." Faith is not that "I got a backup." Real faith is when, "I have no idea *how* this is going to get done, but I trust and believe that it will." I am talking about that real kind of faith. That faith that starts out dry, but by the time you finish praying you've sweated out all your clothes. I'm talking about the kind of faith where you can't pray pretty. You go into prayer with good hair and come out with your true identity showing. That kind of faith is good to have but hard to get.

I heard a Pastor say, how are you going to call yourself a Christian while you are living from paycheck to paycheck? I was like oh, hold on now. I understand the concept but don't put us in hell because things are tight. Don't beat the people up because they are living paycheck to paycheck and then you ask them to give? They're making a sacrifice to give.

God has to sustain us. You have to be careful what atmosphere you create. I have colleagues who don't want to be part of a denomination anymore. But they can't voice it because the church was founded that way and if they were to take the denominational walls down now, they feel they would lose everybody in there.

I had a colleague who trained his people to not believe in speaking in tongues. He was preaching and got the Holy Ghost and had to turn around to speak in tongues because if they had seen it they would have left the church. If the people who hired him had known what happened to him they would have fired him. The next time he got the Holy Ghost he had to run out of the pulpit to the basement of the

Church to speak in tongues. When God wants you he's going to get you. When God wants to get your attention, it doesn't matter where you are he's going to get your attention. Although we need each other, ultimately it's God that sustains us.

The first experience I had speaking in tongues, or having the Holy Ghost, I was watching "The Color Purple." The sisters started singing in their church, "God Is Trying to Tell You Something." I was sitting on the phone talking to my (now) wife, trying to be cool while lying on the couch with a Jerri Curl bag on my head when all of a sudden I had a little feeling *within;* and I got to choking up a little bit like my son Jacob did one night while watching The Secret Life of Bees. Then all of a sudden my lips started shaking and I'm like "heeeey." My body started reacting to this thing. I jumped up, and tried to make it out the room so that nobody could see what was coming. I collapsed outside because someone was in the bathroom, and I couldn't get in. Even though the house was small, this was the run of my life. I collapsed and cried like a baby on the floor.

I remembered thinking, "Oh, I got to get my life right Lord." I haven't been to Church. If I went to church and touched water everything would start smoking. I was just messed up. The power of God shook me on that couch and I tried to run out and it captured me. I crumbled and cried like a baby, and my Mama put the word out, "That boy's on dope. Something is wrong with him." They had no idea that

DON'T THROW AWAY YOUR CONFIDENCE

I had been filled with the Holy Spirit. Church was daycare for my Mama. "You all get on the Church bus." She didn't get on with us because that's when she took a break, but she sent us.

A television personality and me were talking about it years later. He wanted to interview me, and he asked so "you were watching the Color Purple when you got it the first time?" I said, "I didn't know what *"it"* was, but I had something."

And the second time I got my life together and got saved was when a Bishop took me to Manpower, where we stayed all day. You couldn't have told me that so many men were saved. I walked up in there and he told me it's a men's church service. I'm like okay, I'll go. I thought there aren't going to be but twenty people when we get here. Coming from where I was, there weren't that many men around, let alone in church. So I went and we walked up in there and I see all these men and some of them were my age. I was like whoa. I'm not speaking from where I am now; I'm talking about how a young twenty-year-old guy from the streets of Detroit felt about being around all of these Christians. I sat through the service, then later tried to get out of it after they had the nerve to tell me we were going to take a break and have a foot washing. Now that's wrong. That's wrong to a man who won't even touch someone else. That's too intimate, and now you are going to sit me across from somebody I don't even know and tell me I have to wash his foot? Now, see that's like cussing in church.

I told everybody I wouldn't do it. I looked at my Pastor at the time and he said, "don't run." When you are fully submitted to your leader the stuff you wouldn't do for anybody else, you'll do for him or her. Anybody else would have gotten punched. I'd be punching, crying and screaming. You know when you get emotional sometimes and that kind of stuff comes out. I just sat there man. I was like; I've got to touch this foot. This just doesn't make any sense. They got to foot washing. I got to foot washing. Tears starting flowing and I'm like, "Lord, have mercy! What's going on? They're killing me. I feel so violated. This isn't right." They took me back upstairs and the power of God hit that place again. All these warriors, they didn't look like men they looked like warriors now, worshiping God. And I'm like "Lord, have mercy, what is going on!" And I didn't know about all this glory. He took me back home and we're sitting in front of the house on the opposite side of the street. He began to pray saying, "you want the Holy Ghost?" I said, "yeah." Man I got to praying and speaking in tongues and it was over. I had a visitation years earlier that was setting me up for that day. The power of God hit me and arrested me, and I learned from that day on how to trust him.

Everything I just explained to you up to that point was just that I didn't trust. I received a touch; I was able to open myself up. I was guarded. Even during the foot washing, "hey there is something not right with this." The Holy Ghost hit me. Now I'm open. Why? I didn't have a choice. Everything that could have happened did happen. And when the Holy Ghost arrested me, I was open to finding out that God was going to take care of me.

I became convinced that God was going to be my helper I thank God for the prayers of others, but I've got to believe them for myself. If you put anything before God, you're going to be in trouble. If you start looking to yourself instead of God life will trouble you. It always has to be Him first. Everything you do in life has to be unto Him. Everything you do for each other has to be unto Him. Everything you do for me has to be unto Him. Everything has to be unto God. He has to be first.

"The Lord sustains them on their sickbed and restores them from their bed of illness." (Psalm 41:3)

Am I convinced? On my sick bed I had to trust that God was going to sustain me. The prayers of the righteous availed much. Do I want people to pray for me? Of course, I never turn down prayer, just ask my wife. My baby boy can say, "Daddy, let me pray for you." I don't care how tired I am, I say okay. I just don't believe in turning down a prayer.

So I believe that God will sustain me on my sick bed. I believed, and he restored me from my bed of illness. So am I convinced that God will help? Yes!

"*I call out to the Lord, and he answers me from his holy mountain. I lie down and sleep; I wake again, because the Lord sustains me. I will not fear though tens of thousands assail me on every side.*" (Psalm 3:4-6)

What does it mean to sustain? The Lord provides nourishment and all the necessities of my life. So when I lie down and sleep then wake up again, I trust the reason I lied down and was able to get up was because God got me up. I will not fear the tens of thousands drawn against me on every side because God nourishes me. He takes care of me. He protects me. He's my everything.

What comforts me is the fact that there is a God. There are things in your life that probably give you comfort even though they're of no use to you. That's why people drink and do drugs. Comfort, but no use. People gamble, they buy a lottery ticket and won't even redeem it to see if they won because the hope of winning will sustain them for a while. But it's a false hope and they won't trust God. When I did street evangelism, I'd have people pour out their liquor on the street. Anyone who knows me and has been out with me knows that I have no problem requesting those things when I witness. I have no collar on, just jeans whatever; when I'm done they're going to turn that bottle over to me.

So, don't exercise false hopes by trusting in man's system. You've heard me say it before. You don't trust in men. I've said this while the economy was doing well. I said listen, don't trust in man's system. I'm trying to help you get accustomed to doing things God's way.

Are you convinced that God will help? All right, you said it, now you're going to have to prove it. I was going through a tough time financially. Everybody was coming at me. I was months and months behind on my bills. I didn't hide my car. I didn't do any of that. Some people let me down and didn't come through. As I encouraged others I would tell them that I was fine. I said whatever God is doing it's for my benefit. It hurt. I mean I went through some things that were totally demonic because it all happened at the same time. I would roll off of one hit and then get another one. While dealing with one issue, I looked up, and they had broken into my store. I mean it was one thing after another.

My wife was in the hospital. People were leaving the church. Whatever I had my hands on was getting touched. I said, this couldn't be a coincidence. I would confess, "Whatever the enemy is doing let him finish." *Although I went through persecution, I never gave up*. The devil was on me, he was hitting everything, and I just had to believe God. I couldn't get in my flesh about it. I had to pray, cry and pray some more. Friends forsook me, but I trusted in God.

I knew it was God, I knew God was in it for this reason: the minute my breakthrough month came, everything came back at the same time. *I recovered all!* It was so freaking weird. People who had denied and rejected me were calling out the blue. "Remember that money you needed four months ago? I got it now." And then the next call and then the next call. It was hard to believe this was happening. That's how I knew God had finally allowed me to come out of it. That was the time that things just started rolling in. But I had to go through this thing for about two to three years. That's a long time.

So I don't let people judge me because they weren't here when my wife was dying and I was dying and people were leaving and things were falling apart. There were days I couldn't even get out of bed and would listen to her cry all night long in pain. I don't let anybody judge me on how God is blessing us now, because they don't know what we went through.

Try to go home after Church and have people shooting each other in the alley. My children were walking one of the young ladies home and a guy who had just murdered somebody runs right past them on a Sunday after I'd finished preaching. But I trusted The Lord and He kept us. So when I minister to you about what he can do it's not just because I'm trying to encourage you. It's because it's real.

Are you ready for victory?

DON'T THROW AWAY YOUR CONFIDENCE

When you are a willing vessel God can now really use you because ultimately God wants souls. So you are going to have to be the poster boy/poster girl, you have to be first partakers. You know how I know you all are coming out? Because the head comes out first. In the deliverance process, of a natural birth the head has to come out first. If the head doesn't come out first the baby is breeched. God doesn't breach contracts; he fulfills them. Your deliverance is next! I know you're a little wrinkly and it's a little tight right now and you feel like you can't breathe, but in due season you're going to come out. You may cry for a while, but after everything calms down and you're settled, enjoy the comforts of the Holy Spirit.

10 But may[a] the God of all grace, who called us[b] to His eternal glory by Christ Jesus, after you have suffered a while, perfect, establish, strengthen, and settle you. (NKJV) **1 Peter 5:10**

What does sustain mean? To nourish, take care of the necessities of your life.

"He trains my hands for battle; my arms can bend a bow of bronze. You make your saving help my shield, and your right hand sustains me; your help has made me great. You provide a broad path for my feet, so that my ankles do not give way." (Psalm 18:34-36)

"He trains my hands for battle. My arms can bend a bow of bronze. You give me your shield of victory and your right hand sustains me. You stoop down to make me great. You broaden the path beneath me so that my ankles don't turn." **What you're going through is God preparing you for whatever you have got to be engaged in.**

Don't ever forget that you are a spiritual warrior who's never off duty. Take and apply "your" experiences to "your" life. Then, walk in the principles that were just incorporated in you.

Gird up. You're a spiritual warrior.

Faith without works is dead. What's the principle?

Faith cometh by hearing, and hearing by the Word of God. What I've learned, I've got to activate.

I was in a church years ago when a prophet walked up to a guy standing next to me and I was the youth Pastor. He walks up to the guy and said; "I see you working with kids. You're going to be a youth Pastor in this church." I'm standing there like whoa. Did this joker just demote me, because he didn't know me? I didn't know that the church was going to break up and I was going to leave.

So sometimes you hear things and don't know why they are being said. Leave it alone. So God is saying are you ready for victory? He says prove me - try me - challenge me - if I won't open up the windows of Heaven and pour you out a blessing....

[10] The thief does not come except to steal, and to kill, and to destroy. I have come that they may have life, and that they may have *it* more abundantly. (NKJV) **John 10:10**

So, the third principle gives me an indication that God is actually preparing us for victorious living. Jesus said, *"I came that you might have life, and have it more abundantly."* (John 10:10) He doesn't want you to suffer with sickness and disease and worry about bills and all this. And if you think this is an issue unique to only you, then you're missing God.

So God says if you still trust in me, if you believe in me it's going to bring you to a place of victory. I want you to go back and say these three principles again:

1. I am willing to be a vessel used by God.

2. I'm convinced that God will help me and

3. I'm ready for victory.

Put God in remembrance of his promises concerning your life - not that he's forgotten but that you don't forget. Praise God!

J. Richard Evans Sr.

Chapter 6

All Sustaining Power

"Come to me, all you who are weary and burdened, and I will give you rest. Take my yoke upon you and learn from me, for I am gentle and humble in heart, and you will find rest for your souls. For my yoke is easy and my burden is light." (Matthew 11:28-30)

One of the benefits of being a Christian is that we don't have the same mentality as the non-believer when we go through trials. **We are to live according to a standard within the confines of hope.** So whatever I'm experiencing, whatever my neighbor is experiencing, and whatever society is experiencing, the Christian has hope that we are not going to perish in whatever we are dealing with.

When I was coming up, one of the knocks for my not coming to Christ was my observation of Christians who did not act like Christians. My attitude would be, "if you're going through it and I'm going through it, yet I have composure and you're acting like you're about to lose it, why would I follow your God?" That was my knock against them. They would say "the Lord, the Lord..." but I would look at them and because they were not attractive examples to me,

I didn't want to have any part in what they were doing. So no matter what they said about what God could do, I was looking at them and thinking about my buddies who had composure. They were calm, they were cool, they were collected, I mean even sometimes in the most extreme situations. I was from the streets and we dealt with life and death regularly. But under some of the most extreme circumstances those brothers would roll up a joint, relax, and "handle business." I'm being honest. Let's keep it real. Those brothers would roll up a joint; take a shot and then cock and load and go handle business even though they might not come back. I'm being very honest with you. One of the things I love about having my family in the ministry with me is that I don't have to lie. My testimony is authentic.

So, if my partners under some of the most extreme circumstances were giving me an example of how you're supposed to react when you're going through, then a believer who's talking about what God can do shouldn't panic. Why would I follow them? Why would I change my lifestyle if I feel it's better than the Christian?

12 Let no one despise your youth, but be an example to the believers in word, in conduct, in love, in spirit, in faith, in purity. (NKJV) **1 Timothy 4:12**

The reason a Christian should never throw away their confidence is so they might be an example to those who are losing confidence or need encouragement. So when they come at you and say "you're saying you're going through the same thing that I'm going through" you can say "yes, but I'm not going through *it* the same way you're going through *it*." The Bible teaches:

¹⁶ *Therefore we do not lose heart. Even though our outward man is perishing, yet the inward man is being renewed day by day.(NKJV)* **2 Corinthians 4:16**

So we're not supposed to lose it.

Our spiritual leaders are being attacked constantly because the enemy wants you. **The Devil is after your anointing!** If you smite the Shepherd, you scatter the sheep. He does not want you to live out the fullness of what being saved is about. And then he doesn't want you to be an example to anybody else because who needs salvation? He wants to just knock the wind out of you. He's attacking the family. He's attacking marriages. He's attacking the mindset of leaders. He's attacking health. He's disrupting finances. He's doing all that he can, but he won't win.

⁷ *Therefore submit to God. Resist the devil and he will flee from you. (NKJV)* **James 4:7**

We have to go through as one who believes that there is hope. I have hope. That's what it's all about. You have to understand, whatever it is you're dealing with right now, you're not to throw away your confidence because Christians have hope.

One of the things I want you to wrap your mind around is this: **as long as Christ is, as long as the Holy Ghost flows, as long as the earth remains, you have hope**.

8 If I ascend up into heaven, thou art there: if I make my bed in hell, behold, thou art there. (KJV) **Psalm 139:8**

The word declares, "Even the grave can't hold you." We need to have a mindset of "hope." I encourage you to change your mindset. I'm a firm believer in Romans Chapter 12:

"I beseech you therefore, brethren, by the mercies of God, that you present your bodies a living sacrifice, holy, acceptable to God, which is your reasonable service. And do not be conformed to this world, but be transformed by the renewing of your mind, that you may prove what is that good and acceptable and perfect will of God." (Romans 12:1-2)

We're transformed by the renewing of our minds. Change your mind, change your environment, and your life will change. Do you believe that God is going to change some things for you? If you really believe God is getting ready to change some things for you then you have the correct mindset.

23 Jesus said unto him, If thou canst believe, all things are possible to him that believeth. (KJV) **Mark 9:23**

DON'T THROW AWAY YOUR CONFIDENCE

Your situation is turning around; times might be difficult now, but hold on, keep believing, and watch God move! A double minded man is unstable in all his ways. Nothing he does will prosper. So we have to believe there's hope in whatever we are dealing with.

"Come to me, all you who are weary and burdened, and I will give you rest. Take my yoke upon you and learn from me, for I am gentle and humble in heart, and you will find rest for your souls. For my yoke is easy and my burden is light." (Matthew 11:28-30)

One of the things people do when they come to Christ is they take on the yoke of God in personal worship, but they don't come to Bible study. They don't learn the scriptures. If they do, they are trying to learn whatever they can for personal gain, but they never participate in the corporate worship service. But God says we are to do both. He says take my yoke upon you and learn of me. Why take the yoke? If you are not saved and have not had a Christian experience or are not filled with the Holy Ghost, you won't comprehend the things of God.

"Because the carnal mind is enmity against God; for it is not subject to the law of God, nor indeed can be." (Romans 8:7)

The anointing comes to open me up to learn. *"For I am gentle and lowly in heart, and you will find rest for your souls."* In the worship service we come into contact with Christians who believe there is hope in Christ. We enter an atmosphere filled with faith - all of a sudden we're taking on the yoke of God. We're opening up our spirit to learning of God. We are hearing the word of God through a praise filled atmosphere. *"Faith cometh by hearing, and hearing by the word of God."*

People say "I want faith," but then go through a trial and wonder why they didn't make it out of the trial. *Faith cometh by hearing and hearing by the word of God.* So I need the word of God to be taught to me that I might gain faith so when the trials of life come I can live out my trial, knowing that this trial isn't going to kill me. I've got hope. Why do I have hope? Because I've been taught by the preacher/teacher, by the vessel of God in Bible study, and by the mature saints, that there is hope in God. **I learn that I don't have to throw away my confidence. I learn that I can continue believing in God.**

I am gentle and lowly in heart, you will find rest for your weary soul. The anointing falls on me. I'm open... I begin to learn while going through it, learning there is hope that I'm going to come out of what I'm going through, and my soul finds rest.

There are many components to the soul. Emotions, will, mind, intellect, and your imagination, are all part of your soul. So people come into the Church and say, "God is going to save my soul." Yes, but there are components that you have to work out.

DON'T THROW AWAY YOUR CONFIDENCE

That's why people get offended at certain things you say to them. They are either emotional or analytical. Some men won't receive the word because they're trying to analyze everything – and that's part of the soulish realm.

The Lord says when you come in, you get engulfed by the Spirit or under the anointing in the right environment, then you take His yoke upon you. You open up your spirit-man to be taught to learn of Him. In learning of Him, your faith is increased because faith cometh by hearing the word of God. Your faith is being increased. Your spirit-man is being renewed and your soulish area finds rest.

The soul has to be renewed. God says I'll give rest to these areas. God's trying to give you more of his word and you're racking your brain trying to figure everything out. Your intellect, your mind; and then your will get into play. "But I need to know because I need to work this out." Then you get frustrated and become emotional. And now the mind gets to racing. The soul is not finding any rest because I won't just let go and let God. The first thing the text said was to cast your cares upon The Lord. He'll give you rest. He will give you rest for your weary soul.

"Trust in the Lord with all your heart, and lean not on your own understanding; in all your ways acknowledge Him, And He shall direct your paths." (Proverbs 3:5-6)

God is saying, I want to work with you, but you've got to give me something to work with. Stop trying to figure it out. How are you going to figure it out when you're not sure of what's going on? Give it to God. Operate in your faith.

Once I learn what his word says about whatever I'm dealing with, I can activate my faith and do something about it. Sometimes we get out of sorts. We want to do something but are not sure how. Men are bad at this. Instructions come with the purchase but we're going to put the item together without reading the instructions. "I got this." Then we end up with a whole bunch of leftover pieces because we thought we knew what we were doing. What the instruction manual is telling us is to learn to read first.

15 Study to show thyself approved unto God, a workman that needeth not to be ashamed, rightly dividing the word of truth. (KJV) **2 Timothy 2:15**

I believe this scripture is trying to help. Its saying, "Listen; don't go any further until you read this. Because you don't want to be in a tizzy and all messed up, all you have to do is come to me first."

I'm a father. I've got five children and I often ask them why they didn't come to me with difficult issues. Why didn't you come to me? You're trying to work this situation out on your own. You made it worse, when instead you could have just come to me.

DON'T THROW AWAY YOUR CONFIDENCE

Allow me to share the story of using all of your strength:

>A young boy was walking with his father along a country road. When they came across a very large tree branch the boy asked, "Do you think I could move that branch?"
>
>His father answered, "If you use all your strength, I'm sure you can."
>
>So the boy tried mightily to lift, pull and push the branch but he couldn't move it. Discouraged he said, "Dad, you were wrong. I can't do it."
>
>His dad said, "Try again." This time, as the boy struggled with the branch his father joined him and together they pushed the branch aside.
>
>"Son," the father said, "the first time you didn't use all your strength. You didn't ask me to help." *(Wolpe, 1995)*

And God is telling you whatever you're dealing with, have faith that He's going to work it out. But right now, come to him. You don't stop praying. You don't stop going to Church. You don't stop believing God. Whatever you're dealing with, bring it to God. **God will sustain you. God's going to work it out.**

>*"Stand fast therefore in the liberty by which Christ has made us free, and do not be entangled again*

> with a yoke of bondage. Indeed I, Paul, say to you that if you become circumcised, Christ will profit you nothing. And I testify again to every man who becomes circumcised that he is a debtor to keep the whole law." (Galatians 5:1-3)

We are dealing with Christian liberty. A yoke consists of a wooden bar or frame - you've seen them around the necks of oxen and mules. It's to restrict movement and keep you from being able to function the way you want to. A lot of times it was a punishment. So basically when you hear about this "yoke of bondage" it's talking about whatever it is that's restricting you from moving the way you ought to be able to move.

Stand fast in the Christian liberty by which Christ has made us free. Christian liberty is different from just liberty by itself.

He says stand fast for the liberty in which Christ made us free. In the knowledge of who you are as a disciple of Christ. What does God say about you? What does Christ say about you as it pertains to being saved?

And then it says, and do not be entangled with the yoke of bondage again. So let me paint a picture for you. If I didn't know that I had some freedoms as a result of being a Christian, then I wouldn't exercise them because I don't know. So I come to Church and I learn of God. And in learning of

DON'T THROW AWAY YOUR CONFIDENCE

God I find out what freedoms I have as a result of following him. One of the freedoms I ought to have as a result of following God is being stress-free. I have hope. You're stressed out when you don't feel like you have a way out.

Whatever you're dealing with, don't you feel stressed out, don't you feel that you have a means to deal with it properly or expeditiously? But earlier I said we don't mourn and we don't go through things like those that don't have hope. But you, being a Christian have the freedom of being stress-free, knowing that whatever you're dealing with, whatever you're going through or confronting as a Christian, you're not supposed to struggle as those who have no hope. For a man who faints in a day of adversity his strength is small. Therefore, if you really have been studying your Bible, you really have been living a moral life and believing God, then you ought to be a little bit stronger today than you were this time last year.

As you go through life and apply what you've learned about God to what you are going through, you become stronger dealing with those kinds of situations.

Listen, don't let anybody tell you that isn't true. That's like saying if you start lifting weights and stay faithful and don't quit and keep that regimen going for six weeks you're going to be weaker. That would be a foolish statement. The law of physics says that you're going to get stronger. This principle works. The more life comes at you, the stronger you are going to get dealing with life while believing in God.

I don't go through a day the way I used to go through it. If you've got somebody who is still as fragile today as they were five or six years ago and they were saved, something is wrong. It's like someone who says they workout, however, there are no results. You look at them and say "you're just as flabby six years later." It doesn't add up. You don't see the results of what they are confessing.

4 I therefore, the prisoner of the Lord, beseech you that ye walk worthy of the vocation wherewith ye are called, (KJV) **Eph. 4:1**

I'm a Pastor, but I'm a Christian first. Anybody you meet from 5-fold ministries, Bishops, Apostles, Pastors, Preachers, Teachers, Evangelists, Prophets, whatever the title, they are still Christians first. Often, we get a title and think we no longer need to work to remain Christians. When this happens you end up with faulty leaders who are really just faulty Christians. I'm still a Christian. I'm a Christian first, and so as a Christian I'm still required to study my word, read my word and apply what I learn to my life. Being a Pastor doesn't give me a free pass.

12 Wherefore, my beloved, as ye have always obeyed, not as in my presence only, but now much more in my absence, work out your own salvation with fear and trembling. (KJV) **Philippians 2:12**

Sometimes the world views you the way you view Preachers or Pastors. The world looks at you when you got saved as if you should have gotten a pass on life. "If you're saved, why are you looking for a job like me?" Just because I got saved doesn't give me a pass on jobs. I still have to eat. I still have to pay bills.

My desire is for a corporate manifestation of the revelation of God's Providence for the believer. We want divine guidance and care. God is the Power sustaining and guiding our respective destinies. We need to be reminded of who we are. If every individual takes that revelation and applies it to their situation, their future gets brighter. You just teach that person how to function in whatever situation they find themselves in, they're going to work that system and get their desired outcome.

"So if I give you these principles and you learn to apply them to whatever situation you get in, you are able to navigate through life. It doesn't matter if it's money, faith, faithfulness, courage, strength, or whatever it is, I must understand the key principle is that whatever I'm going through, **I must first go to God**. While God is teaching me His essence, his way, then my soulish realm is being comforted so that once I learn what to do about it, I begin to activate my faith, knowing that whatever I'm going through there's hope that I'm coming out. My mindset begins to change and as a result my environment begins to change, and by the time I take inventory my whole life has changed.

"I am writing these things to you about those who are trying to lead you astray. As for you, the anointing you received from him remains in you, and you do not need anyone to teach you. But as his anointing teaches you about all things and as that anointing is real, not counterfeit—just as it has taught you, remain in him. And now, dear children, **continue in him, so that when he appears we may be confident and unashamed before him at his coming."** (1 John 2:26-28)

Remember, you do not need anyone to teach you what you've already learned because the anointing still remains in you, which in turn causes you to retain what you've already learned. And his anointing teaches you about all things. And as that anointing is real and not counterfeit - what he taught you not only remains in you, but also is still real in him.

I have people coming to get counsel from me and after I give it they come back and say all right, tell me again. I told somebody one time what they really want is for me to change my mind, because if I were to change my mind, then my counsel changes. In other words *"I don't want to follow what you told me to do. It doesn't work for me. Give me a different recipe."* At times like this you have to stick to your guns and say, "No, I already told you what works. You need to follow what works."

So if God is going to give me an anointing that destroys yokes of bondage that come to restrict me from moving like I should as a Christian and restrict me from believing like I should believe as a Christian, whatever it is - there has to be an anointing that comes upon me to enable me to destroy whatever that distraction is. It takes us all the way back to Matthew 11:28. ²⁸ Come to Me, all *you* who labor and are heavy laden, and I will give you rest. (NKJV)

People often quit Church before they can learn anything and then try to make you follow them. Not me. Don't quit prematurely. Don't give up just yet.

"Come to me, all you who are weary and burdened, and I will give you rest. Take my yoke upon you and learn from me, for I am gentle and humble in heart, and you will find rest for your souls. For my yoke is easy and my burden is light." (Matthew 11:28-30)

I take his yoke when I get submerged in his atmosphere and become submerged in the spirit. I'm opening up my spirit to learn from God and this destroys the yokes of bondage that would try to lead me in a different direction.

These yokes come from teachings that are not going to help me get out of what I'm going through because they don't line up with the word of God. And there are personalities that will try to get me to follow them by petting my flesh because it feels good. What I'm getting from God might not feel good, but it is good.

So if I submerge myself in an atmosphere of worship, praise, prayer, faith and belief, it breaks the yoke of bondage that would try to pull me out before God pulls me up.

I need to make sure that I'm engulfed in an atmosphere that will cause these yokes to be broken in my life. The anointing destroys yokes of bondage.

"And now, dear children, continue in him, so that when he appears we may be confident and unashamed before him at his coming." (1 John 2:28)

Whatever you're going through in life, start being the kind of person that sees it through and don't try to get out of what you're dealing with prematurely but be willing to see it through.

² My brethren, count it all joy when you fall into various trials, ³ knowing that the testing of your faith produces patience. ⁴ But let patience have its perfect work, that you may be perfect and complete, lacking nothing. ⁵ If any of you lacks wisdom, let him ask of God, who gives to all liberally and without reproach, and it will be given to him. ⁶ But let him ask in faith, with no doubting, for he who doubts is like a wave of the sea driven and tossed by the wind. ⁷ *For let not that man suppose that he will receive anything from the Lord; ⁸ he is a double-minded man, unstable in all his ways. (NKJV)* ***James 1:1-8***

James 1 teaches us that we're to count it all joy when we encounter trials because the trying of your faith produces patience. It didn't say reading, it said knowing. This is the problem we seem to have. We start going through something and try to figure out what's going on. But if you were built up on faith from the last time you went through a trial, by now you would be convinced and you would know that you could make it.

If someone says "I'm going to send you a check in the mail," you say Ok and you don't sweat it. You don't get nervous, and you don't rack your brain because you've used the mail system before and in your mind the mail is going to be delivered. It's a proven system. So if I really want to walk in my Christian freedoms I've got to get to a place where I trust God and have confidence in *His* system. It might not start the same day you get saved, but after operating in it a while, trials can't shake me the way they use to. I can handle them better now.

I'm certain that you've been tried, but some were smaller in comparison to others. Looking back, I'm sure you don't even look on it, as being a challenge because it wasn't severe enough to move you. It comes, you deal with it and you go on. It's like the TV being fuzzy because of poor reception; you check the connection to clear the channel. You don't even think about it. You don't sit there racking your brain. It was a trial wasn't it? It kind of distorts your view, messes your time up and messes with your program. What did you do? Secured the connection and continued watching your show, not realizing that it was really a trial, but it wasn't severe enough to cause you any major concerns because you corrected it just like that.

Some trials require a little bit more of your energy than others. How you deal with it makes the difference, but it's building up your faith.

"And now, dear children, continue in him, so that when he appears we may be confident and unashamed before him at his coming." (John 2:28)

He's talking about the children of God and their being able to identify those who belong to him. When He appears, he's coming for a church without spot or wrinkle. He says you've got to have confidence. Did it say hide in him? No, it said abide in him. Christians want to hide. He didn't say hide in him. He said abide in him. It's a different mindset. When you go to your home, your house, you're not hiding, you're abiding. It's a mindset.

If somebody were after me I might have to run in for refuge. I might have to hide if I think they're coming to get me. But because I'm not on the run when I go home I'm abiding. So a lot of times Christians think "I'm getting saved I can hide in him." Now, I know we've all read the scriptures about hiding in God... We're not talking about that. I'm abiding and exercising Christian authority. I'm going to enjoy my life. You all want to enjoy your lives don't you?

I don't know about you, but although I might not be the brightest bulb in the box, I'm not crazy enough to follow something that doesn't work. I don't know about the rest of you, but I'm not scared. I'm not hiding in God. People who hide in God might not believe anything that he's going to do and find themselves too scared to confront the world, so they just hide. "Oh you better not believe like that." Why not? The Bible says that I can. You understand we don't have to beg and be scared all the time. I have a lot of reverence for God, but I know what God said, faith without works is dead. I've got to apply what I've been reading to my life in order for it to be activated and work for me. **I'm not hiding. I'm abiding.**

Speak to anything that's messing with you in your life. Speak to it. Don't wait until you get to Church. Don't wait to call the saints. Rebuke the spirit that's trying to mess with your family. If the devil knows that you're waiting to be rescued, you're in trouble. He's going to get everybody distracted.

I'm not ashamed. I'm confident. *"So that when he appears we may be confident unashamed before him at his coming."* Now I know this is talking about the latter times, but listen. If I don't start practicing it where I am now, I'm not going to be ready when he shows up. So I have to start practicing this thing now. You have to be confident.

When my confidence begins to wane, you know what I do? I pray first, then I call the saints.

"Not forsaking the assembling of ourselves together, as is the manner of some, but exhorting one another, and so much the more as you see the Day approaching." (Hebrews 10:25)

There's encouragement in this. When you get among the saints you don't even realize how much power you've got. Seriously, you haven't folded yet.

Chapter 7

Don't Be Insecure

"Come to me, all you who are weary and burdened, and I will give you rest. Take my yoke upon you and learn from me, for I am gentle and humble in heart, and you will find rest for your souls. For my yoke is easy and my burden is light." (Matthew 11:28-30)

In the previous chapter we ministered on how God was our all-sustaining power, but in this chapter we are going to deal with insecurity.

To be insecure is to be anxious or lacking in self-confidence. A person who's not confident is not safe, and is unstable. They aren't firm or steady.

"Consider it pure joy, my brothers and sisters, whenever you face trials of many kinds, because you know that the testing of your faith produces perseverance. Let perseverance finish its work so that you may be mature and complete, not lacking anything. If any of you lacks wisdom, you should ask God, who gives generously to all without finding fault, and it will be given to you. But when you ask, you must believe and not doubt, because the one who doubts is like a wave of the sea, blown and tossed by the wind.

That person should not expect to receive anything from the Lord. Such a person is double-minded and unstable in all they do." (James 1:2-7)

If you're dealing with anybody who's insecure, they're not going to profit you anything. Did you hear what James said? He said if you're going to have confidence in anything pertaining to God you can't be double minded, you can't be fickle, you can't be unstable.

I cannot be so insecure that I attack everything around me that I consider to be a threat. You've been making it all this time and all of a sudden you yoke up with someone who wants to restructure everything you've been standing on to survive because of their insecurities. God says no.

Nelson Rockefeller wrote *"you are a child of God. Your playing small does not serve the world. There is nothing enlightened about shrinking so that other people won't feel insecure about you. We were born to manifest the glory of God that is within us."*

That's a powerful statement, from a powerful man. What has crept into your life that's trying to restructure you and cause you to fail because of insecurities?

⁷ You ran well. Who hindered you from obeying the truth? (NKJV)**Galatians 5:7**

DON'T THROW AWAY YOUR CONFIDENCE

I've been married for over 23 years. I told a friend of mine a long time ago, "Man, I have never hid in the bushes trying to find out what my wife is doing when I'm not around." I've been with her for a long time. I'm a secure man. I'm a secure leader and I like to have secure people around me.

The Book of James says: a double minded man is insecure. This also applies to anybody who is fickle - here today, gone tomorrow. People who can't make up their minds, he says they are insecure, and insecure people don't profit.

The danger of being insecure is that it creates a feeling of either low or no self-esteem. When you have a feeling of low or no self-esteem you are always under threat. You feel that you're under attack and that people are coming against you. Insecure people destroy themselves. Anytime success stares them in the face they find a reason to attack it because of their own insecurities.

Insecurities can be defined as a lack of trust in anything or any person you have to depend on; depression; or shyness. Some causes of insecurities are:

- Employment

- Relationships

- Poor social skills

- Finances

- Self-esteem

- Fear of a challenge or anything new

- Fear of change

All of these are ways insecurities can be manifested. Can anybody identify with any of that?

When you have feelings of insecurity you doubt yourself and your ability to cope with the problem or situation, or you fear a negative outcome. Whatever arises, because of insecurity you can never confront it the way it needs to be confronted because you never look at it through the right viewfinder. Insecurity is really the same thing as low self-confidence.

What can you do then if you feel insecure?

Addressing the problem is very important as insecurity can develop into something even worse and become genuine fear or even panic which will cause you to avoid difficult situations. Rather than avoid these situations you should confront them and learn to overcome them.

I've said before, some people can never find success because they are so insecure that the minute any opposition creeps up they get defensive and start attacking whatever it is that could be a blessing.

If you experience insecurity and lack of confidence in any situation, first ask yourself if there is any logical reason for your feelings. If you feel insecure about anything, or just think about some of the things you feel insecure about, did you ever stop and ask yourself why you're so scared? Have you ever faced a fear and instead of freaking out and panicking, you pause for a minute and asked now why am I scared? What's really going to happen?

Think about our phobias: things that really cause us to shudder with fear. Have you ever thought what could really happen?

It's not logical for me to watch TV and see an image of looking down from a great height and get dizzy but it happens, even though it's not logical. How are you ever going to get anywhere in Christ if you're not thinking logically and are afraid to get over your fears?

I'm the guy who hops on the airplane and sits in the window seat because I would rather confront my fears of flying and be successful than allow it to overtake me and act all irrational. It's still there, but I'm willing to confront it. I didn't say I liked it. I didn't say it didn't bother me, I said I can't stand to fly, but I will get on a plane in a minute because I'm not insecure.

This is what logic says to me: "There are more people crashing in cars everyday than in planes." I know you're saying people who have automobile accidents don't always die, but people who crash in planes don't always die either. Logically, planes are safer than cars. So logic can help you.

But what about the scripture that says *"lean not to thine own understanding, but in all thy ways acknowledge Him and He'll make straight your paths."*

If I grab ahold of God and my belief in him to keep the pilot, the plane and me then I can overcome my fear. This is going to help you because sometimes you don't even realize you're already living defeated or you let people come into your life who live defeated and they chip away at your confidence little by little. They say, "I don't know why you feel like that. I don't know why you have so much confidence. I don't know why you believe like that. I don't know why you've got that much faith."

The reason they feel that way is because they're experiencing a lack of confidence. Maybe they never identified what they were dealing with because they couldn't see beyond where they were. Somebody you respect has to come into your life and say, "listen, do you know what you're really dealing with?" You cannot allow yourself to let insecurity overtake you.

It's a skill you need to develop in order to be prepared for the challenges of life. In this case you can solve your sense of insecurity simply by watching others or learning the skills necessary to be confident in the situation you fear.

DON'T THROW AWAY YOUR CONFIDENCE

Connect with someone emotionally healthy. If you're dealing with an insecure person, before you can get healthy they will chip away at your self-esteem because they are too weak to handle a strong personality.

When God is trying to develop you, be careful not to yoke up, befriend, or make a covenant with somebody who chips away at your confidence.

Sometimes insecure people will chip away at the truth because they don't understand it, and you don't realize what you're dealing with. I was at a corporate meeting one time and this certain person was talking gibberish. The executives were all on the edge of their seats because he was supposedly an expert in his field. I said, just because he's talking a lot doesn't mean he knows what he's talking about. Nobody said anything, or questioned him. Nobody took down any notes because they were just on the edge of their seats. He was talking gibberish. I knew him, and I knew his game.

So I learned a long time ago that you better watch who you hook up with. If that person is insecure, before you get your breakthrough, they will have chipped away at what was trying to break you out.

Maybe you were stronger at one time, but now there is something wrong with your walk. There was a time when you were stronger emotionally, but now there is something wrong with you. Whatever I hook up with, whatever I befriend, whatever I covenant with comes to make me better, not to tear me down. Who gave you the authority to tear me down? Who gave you the authority to come into my life and disrupt it and not make it better? Who gave you the authority to come here and mess with my confidence?

Don't mess up my confidence; don't tear me up to get me to change. Be patient with me and give me time. You're wondering why I'm going through the same stuff that got me to be who I am, it's because you're killing it. Give me time to transition to be better, but don't tear me up in the process.

There is a skill to overcoming insecurity. Everything that you deal with has to be developed. There is a difference between being confident and being cocky.

If a certain system works better for you then let the system work. I can say this and be successful. You have to be a secure person to be able to handle it.

[18] *There is no fear in love; but perfect love casts out fear, because fear involves torment. But he who fears has not been made perfect in love. (NKJV)* **1 John 4:18**

Did you know worrying is a sin. Insecure people worry a lot, even when you give them the answer. Have you ever noticed that? Don't worry this is taken care of. *You sure?*

One of the manifestations of insecurity is shyness. Shyness is a big problem, but if you face it you can overcome it.

⁶Be anxious for nothing, but in everything by prayer and supplication, with thanksgiving, let your requests be made known to God; (NKJV) **Phil. 4:6**

Sometimes we don't want to confront certain things because we're too shy. What happens when what you need to overcome is going to make your life better, but you're too shy to confront it? Often it's not the devil that has to be overcome, it's you. You can't ever honestly say the devil made you do anything.

¹³There hath no temptation taken you but such as is common to man: but God is faithful, who will not suffer you to be tempted above that ye are able; but will with the temptation also make a way to escape, that ye may be able to bear it. (KJV) **1 Cor. 10:13**

So if you confront these challenges and don't run from them, your life can be better. Remember, this is a world filled with dangers, worries and insecurities.

Most people around the world fear terrorism and are stressed about so many aspects of their lives. Modern life seems to be removed from us, so we are not as relaxed as we used to be and life seems to be slowing down. Would you agree to that? A lot of people won't even dare get on a plane since September 11th.

But listen you are not alone. There are a lot of people who feel the same way, the difference is they have gotten over these insecurities. You have to learn to talk to people and hear differences of opinions. Friends are a great help in this respect, if they're real friends.

Whatever you feel insecure about, talk about it calmly and improve your skills in dealing with it, then confront it and you will succeed. If you're insecure, confess it.

[16] *Confess your trespasses to one another, and pray for one another, that you may be healed. The effective, fervent prayer of a righteous man avails much. (NKJV)* **James 5:16**

Begin to work on improving your skills in dealing with it before you confront it. It's important you get that.

Sometimes we confront things out of panic. We did not calmly bring it up. We did not learn to deal with it prior to confronting it and now we're wondering why it became a bigger mess. We're talking about not throwing away our confidence now. So I must identify my issue. *This is the problem I'm having and we need to work on it.* After we start working on it I get better. I get stronger and now I'm ready to confront it.

[20] *for the wrath of man does not produce the righteousness of God. (NKJV)* **James 1:20**

I don't have a problem saying I don't like to fly. You notice I don't use the word fear. I do not say I have a fear of flying. I don't confess that. I say I don't like to fly. But I understand that in order to confront it I've got to deal with it. So I buy a ticket. I haven't flown ten hours in one direction yet, but I'm working on it. I'm going to go to Hawaii soon, but right now five hours is my max. I've been as far away as California. I've been to other countries on three and four hour flights. I can handle those three and four hour flights. I've mastered it by going to sleep. I book my flight early in the morning, around sleep time. The flight leaves at 6 a.m. and I'm going to sleep two hours while the rest of the time I read a book.

Now there have been flights I've been on where somebody slipped me caffeine and I had to stay up the whole time reading or praying. *Talk about getting close to the Lord.* I didn't know I could pray that many hours straight. I fly all the time. I have to work on Africa though. All that water too? Because now my prayer has to be, Lord, I believe I'm going to stay up in the air, but if we happen to hit water give me the ability to hold onto the whale, the shark or whatever. Let me tell you something, I'm riding something. You can sit up there and let a shark bite you if you want but I'm not fighting him. I'm trying to get on his head. I'm riding. Take something off and wrap it in his mouth. I'll lasso it.

I was talking to someone, and they said we have to fly over the Everglades and I'm like *"And..., Remember I told you that joke?* I said I'll be the black guy riding the alligator. Who is that? Evans. They'll be like, what are you doing? *Riding my shoes until they get tired." (laughing)*

When you have to do public speaking they say find somebody and picture them... well we can't do that because we're saved, but find somebody and picture a humorous scene. Focus on them and you can speak calmly. If you start doing this, this stuff is funny but if you were on a plane and you thought *"man, Pastor was talking about riding an alligator."* Wouldn't something humorous like that ease your nerves?

Submit to God, Resist the Devil

⁵ Likewise you younger people, submit yourselves to your elders. Yes, all of you be submissive to one another, and be clothed with humility, for

"God resists the proud, But gives grace to the humble."[a]

⁶ Therefore humble yourselves under the mighty hand of God, that He may exalt you in due time,

DON'T THROW AWAY YOUR CONFIDENCE

⁷ casting all your care upon Him, for He cares for you. (NKJV) **1 Peter 5:5-7**

The confident get around certain people that are confident. We were going through the security checkpoint one time and one of my colleagues said he was going to wear his clergy collar because maybe they wouldn't check him. Not only did they check him, they stripped him all the way down. We had a little fun with that. Man, I wore regular stuff. So we talk about that kind of stuff to keep us from getting upset going through airport security. Hang around people that are confident like that. Not insecure.

The Race of Faith

12 Therefore we also, since we are surrounded by so great a cloud of witnesses, let us lay aside every weight, and the sin which so easily ensnares us, and let us run with endurance the race that is set before us, ² looking unto Jesus, the author and finisher of our faith, who for the joy that was set before Him endured the cross, despising the shame, and has sat down at the right hand of the throne of God.

The Discipline of God

³ For consider Him who endured such hostility from sinners against Himself, lest you become weary and discouraged in your souls. (NKJV) **Heb. 12:1-29**

We have to learn not to be so insecure that we think everything around us that's not like us is a threat.

2 Do not forget to entertain strangers, for by so doing some have unwittingly entertained angels. (NKJV) **Heb. 13:2**

I thought you were more confident. Doesn't it feel good to be confident and know you've got God in your life? People actually like to be around you.

Self-confidence is something you can have and this will help you move closer to the life you feel you should have. Without confidence and self-esteem you cannot easily achieve what you want. I didn't say you couldn't achieve it. I said you couldn't achieve it easily.

Christian Liberty

5 Stand fast therefore in the liberty by which Christ has made us free,[a] and do not be entangled again with a yoke of bondage. (NKJV) **Galatians 5:1**

It's very important that we say the word easily, because you can still achieve it. There are a lot of insecure people that achieve great amounts of success but they didn't do it easily.

Listen carefully when people start making excuses. You're in a good Church. Things are going well. You get nervous. Nobody knows. There was a sermon that was preached that was challenging. Nobody really knows what triggers your insecurities, but all of a sudden you go into self-destruct mode. *Maybe they don't love me. Nobody likes me. They hate me.*

What if Peter said that about Jesus because Jesus saw greatness in him and challenged him more than anybody else? What if Peter started saying *Jesus doesn't like me. He hates me. I quit.*

J. Richard Evans Sr.

Chapter 8

Don't Quit... GET YOUR REWARD!

"Consider it pure joy, my brothers and sisters, whenever you face trials of many kinds, because you know that the testing of your faith produces perseverance. Let perseverance finish its work so that you may be mature and complete, not lacking anything. If any of you lacks wisdom, you should ask God, who gives generously to all without finding fault, and it will be given to you. But when you ask, you must believe and not doubt, because the one who doubts is like a wave of the sea, blown and tossed by the wind. That person should not expect to receive anything from the Lord. Such a person is double-minded and unstable in all they do." (James 1:2-7)

In the last chapter we brought out some of the troubles with being insecure. One of the troubles with insecurity is that those who are insecure usually sabotage the success of their own relationships. An insecure person will be in a secure relationship on their way to success, but because of insecurities they jeopardize the success of that relationship.

I'm speaking from experience. I struggled my entire childhood with insecurities. I grew up poor, the product of a broken home, the middle son to a single mother. I have struggles that I've never discussed in an open setting, and challenges that I've only confessed to God. I've lived with the scars and wounds of mistakes too numerous to list, and too embarrassing to recount. Insecurities? Yeah, I know them all too well. These insecurities made me cower as a child as the target of bullies twice my size and often a few years my senior. They fueled and fed an inner monster that would one day have the courage to reveal itself. I would get to know them all too well: fear, frustration, shyness, anger, hatred, jealousy, murder, and violence. This was my environment, and I learned to adapt to it in hopes of survival.

[13] Brethren, I do not count myself to have apprehended; but one thing I do, forgetting those things which are behind and reaching forward to those things which are ahead, [14] I press toward the goal for the prize of the upward call of God in Christ Jesus. (NKJV) **Philippians 3:13-14**

After the death of my father due to a massive heart attack on May 4, 1984, I began dealing drugs, and insecurity was there. I was angry, bitter, violent and resentful. I had a lack of respect for women, and contempt for all men. I was extremely hateful. With my father no longer there for me to answer to, no longer there for me to fear, I expressed my anger in an attempt to hide my pain. Fear fueled my tough exterior.

DON'T THROW AWAY YOUR CONFIDENCE

Children and Parents

Children, obey your parents in the Lord, for this is right. (NKJV) **Ephesians 6:1**

From the Cradle

How my mother put up with me I will never understand. However, she covered me. I know it was love. I thank God that she never gave up on me. It was my mother's prayers that kept me down through the years.

⁶ *Train up a child in the way he should go: and when he is old, he will not depart from it. (KJV)* **Proverbs 22:6**

I had to learn not to allow insecurity to continue to victimize me. Without the proper guidance and influence in my life, I continued to struggle. I had never been affirmed. No one instructed me on how to conduct myself, no one taught me how to be a man. I had limited social skills. I was suffering and didn't know it. A feeling of insecurity means that your self-esteem will be under threat and may already be suffering. That's why it is so important for you to find security. Have you ever known anybody who sabotages a good thing by always finding fault in that thing because of his or her fear of failing at it?

I've known people over the years that, no matter what relationship they find themselves in, they never succeed at it. They always pointed the finger at everybody else. The common factor in the relationship was them. No matter where they go, there they are.

Could it be that they have a fear of succeeding, like I did?

People have this mentality of "I'm going to quit you before you fire me". *I have never been fired from a job.* Yes, but you quit seventeen of them.

Insecure people tend to victimize the people closest to them. They can be verbally, physically, and emotionally abusive, and in church they can be spiritually abusive.

I'm guilty of learning how to Pastor on the move. One of the things I learned a long time ago is that some things you do as a Pastor that people think is careless, isn't careless, it's just reckless.

I want to bring you to a place of being more careful instead of causing your own destruction. When you have feelings of insecurity you doubt yourself and your abilities to cope with the problems or situation or you fear a negative outcome. Insecurity is really the same thing as low self-confidence or low self-esteem.

What can you do if you feel insecure? I think addressing the problem is really important as insecurities can develop into something worse and become real fear or even panic, which will cause you

DON'T THROW AWAY YOUR CONFIDENCE

to avoid situations you find difficult. Rather than avoid these situations you should confront them and learn to overcome them. Most people never confront their issues, instead they quit, especially in the church.

At the first sign of trouble or challenge, the spirit of fear comes on us, but the Bible states in 2 Timothy 1:7

[7] For God hath not given us the spirit of fear; but of power, and of love, and of a sound mind. (KJV) 2 Timothy 1:7

What gets me is this, who said you failed the last time? Who told you that you failed the last time? Who told you that you messed up the last time? What about the time before that?

When will you confront your fear of failure, or whatever your insecurity is, and be willing to succeed this time, even though you feel like you could fail?

Let me tell you something I've learned; nothing feels better than facing the possibility of failing, but then succeeding. Nothing feels better than confronting an obstacle that you thought would defeat you, but at the end of that thing you came out victorious.

Some of you want to be in a fixed fight. You want to go in with guns loaded on your side so you can just chalk up another victory to pad your record. That really doesn't prepare you for anything. It might boost your confidence for a while, but what will really boost your confidence is when you face something that could have beaten you, but you overcame it. Even though you wanted to run, you chose not to.

Real superheroes don't wear capes. Most superheroes don't transform from Clark Kent to Superman or Wonder woman. Most Superheroes are everyday folks just like you and me who confronted something that should have beaten them, but they overcame it. However, they had to first overcome their own insecurities.

Oftentimes it's not the gift and the talent, it was the insecurity that caused them to run, because they were not able to confront them.

I shared with a class a long time ago that King David in the Old Testament never defeated his giant. And everybody said, "Yes he did. He knocked Goliath off his block, cut his head off and paraded around with it." I said listen, the real giant in David's life wasn't Goliath. The real giant in David's life was himself. David liked women. David couldn't control his own house. So even though he was a public success, he was a private failure. His son raped his daughter. His son raped his own sister, one son got so violently angry he murdered all of his brothers and then came back to kill his own Daddy. He had a problem in his own family with leadership, but he could lead men into battle and kill his tens of thousands and all that, but he could never conquer his own flesh.

He should have been on the battlefield, but instead he was up on the rooftop peeking at Bathsheba. He ended up getting her pregnant and to make sure her husband, Uriah wouldn't know, he told him to come home and leave everybody else at war. Uriah called the regiment in but said I can't go in and sleep with my wife when men under my command cannot do the same thing with their wives. Uriah had more integrity than the king.

Then David said, "I'll tell you what, take him back and put him on the front lines and then have everyone else pull back and leave him to fight the enemy by himself." This is David. This is a man after God's own heart. This is a man that God loved. David had the man killed over his own indiscretions.

This is the same David that when he was old and they thought he was dead, they brought a woman in with him and when he didn't make a move for her they said; the king is dead. In his old age, he still had a lack of self-control. He never conquered his own demons and as a result he gave birth to Solomon, who had three hundred wives and seven hundred concubines. That's a thousand women, and he still ended up sleeping with strange women because he had an insatiable appetite. He could not be satisfied.

But Jesus himself said there would never be another one as wise as Solomon. So if anybody knew better, he did.

What is wisdom by the way? It is knowledge applied. So he had knowledge. He had wisdom. He had understanding, but he still had some issues birthed through insecurities. We have to get to a place where we learn to conquer our own inner demons.

A double-minded man is insecure, unstable in all he does. I don't want to sit in an insecure, unstable chair because it might break and I might fall.

If you were to act on every thought that entered your mind there would be some trouble. So what separates you from a murderer? Reason? Being rational? Casting down those thoughts and any other thing that exalts itself against the knowledge of God.

We have got to learn how to reason. So be reasonable. There are some things that would enter your mind that would try to cause you to go off the deep end. But you know how to cast them down. We're trying to get you to develop yourself to where you learn how to cast down even more unreasonable things.

So you have to be careful that you don't associate with people that you know have the upper hand on you. So I try to surround myself with people who challenge me to be, not just better than what I am, but more of what I am.

Talk to others. Share your concerns.

Whatever it is that you feel insecure about, talk about it calmly and improve your skills in dealing with it and confront it.

Again, confess it, and reason within yourself. Learn from it by dealing with it, and then confront it. Learning from it and confronting it is not the same thing.

I'm going to deal with this, and you go and confront it in the wrong way. Dealing with it is *"I've got to reason, I've got to figure this thing out. Let me mull this over."* Because in dealing with it you begin to work out the scenario in your head. There would be a whole lot of empty prisons if people dealt with it before they confronted it. They never dealt with it, they just confronted the situation without thinking things through. Now they're doing life or in some cases have lost their lives. They go to prison and we go to prison with them. Families are messed up because people had insecurities.

Perhaps you just need to get yourself organized and disciplined. Don't be afraid to seek help if you need it. Self-confidence is something that you should have and it will help you move closer to the life that you feel you should have. Without confidence and self-esteem you can't achieve what you want easily.

We are warriors in the service of our Lord. Any military leader will tell you that a vital element in maintaining an effective fighting force is morale. If the men are confident in their abilities and believe in the possibility of victory then they are a force to be reckoned with. On the other hand, a demoralized soldier with little or no confidence will not be much good in a conflict regardless of his personal training and no matter how good he is. Our ancient foe, the devil knows this, which is why one of the primary weapons in his arsenal is discouragement, which he deploys to destroy our confidence.

Knowing this, you have the choice as to whether you want to give into his wiles or not. God intended for us to walk confidently in the knowledge that through Christ we can do all things and achieve the victory. This does not mean we are cocky, but it is rather an acknowledgement of where our strength comes from. Your morale level is up to you.

So again I humbly say, don't throw away your confidence. Your reward is closer than you realize!

www.ingramcontent.com/pod-product-compliance
Lightning Source LLC
LaVergne TN
LVHW051558070426
835507LV00021B/2641